Driving Performance at Ireland's Commission for Regulation of Utilities

This work is published under the responsibility of the Secretary-General of the OECD. The opinions expressed and arguments employed herein do not necessarily reflect the official views of OECD member countries.

This document, as well as any data and any map included herein, are without prejudice to the status of or sovereignty over any territory, to the delimitation of international frontiers and boundaries and to the name of any territory, city or area.

Please cite this publication as:
OECD (2018), *Driving Performance at Ireland's Commission for Regulation of Utilities*, The Governance of Regulators, OECD Publishing, Paris.
http://dx.doi.org/10.1787/9789264190061-en

ISBN 978-92-64-18994-2 (print)
ISBN 978-92-64-19006-1 (PDF)

Series: The Governance of Regulators
ISSN 2415-1432 (print)
ISSN 2415-1440 (online)

Revised version, February 2017
Details of revisions available at:
http://www.oecd.org/about/publishing/Corrigendum-Driving_Performance_Ireland.pdf

The statistical data for Israel are supplied by and under the responsibility of the relevant Israeli authorities. The use of such data by the OECD is without prejudice to the status of the Golan Heights, East Jerusalem and Israeli settlements in the West Bank under the terms of international law.

Photo credits: Cover © Leigh Prather - Fotolia.com, © Mr.Vander - Fotolia.com, © magann - Fotolia.com.

Foreword

The business of "regulating" is becoming increasingly less technocratic and more sophisticated. Complexity, technological advancement and societal change are transforming the way that regulatory agencies operate. Traditionally tasked with ensuring access to and quality of public services, facilitating investments, and protecting market neutrality, regulators today are dealing with greater demands in a context of uncertainty. They need to be flexible, robust and aware – able to react to new trends, stand up to scrutiny, and actively collect and analyse data and information. Against this backdrop, good governance is all the more essential.

The OECD has developed a framework to help regulators assess and strengthen their organisational performance by looking at both internal and external governance. Internal governance refers to organisational structures, behaviour, accountability, business processes, reporting and performance management; external governance, to the roles, relationships, distribution of powers and responsibilities with other government and non-government stakeholders.

This report applies the OECD framework to the Irish Commission for Regulation of Utilities (CRU), responsible for regulating energy markets, energy safety, and public water and wastewater services in Ireland. The review finds that the CRU is a mature and well-performing regulator that has, among some of its achievements, facilitated Ireland's transition from monopolistic gas and electricity sectors to fully competitive markets, and expanded its regulatory remit to include energy safety, the joint-oversight of the all-island Single Electricity Market between Ireland and Northern Ireland, and water regulation.

While the CRU has successfully adapted to meet its growing mandate, it is also facing a number of new challenges. These include external factors such as Brexit and European energy reforms that add complexity to the future governance of Irish utilities. Moreover, a rapidly transforming market requires the CRU to regulate emerging technologies and to deliver and effectively communicate on increasingly sophisticated products, such as smart meters.

The report recommends a package of integrated reforms to help the CRU prepare for the future. These recommendations are intended to complement the CRU's ongoing efforts to improve its governance processes in line with best practices. The review underlines the importance for the CRU of setting and communicating priorities more assertively as an independent regulator, building its culture of independence internally and with external stakeholders, seeking more flexibility in managing its human resources, better aligning its strategic objectives with resources and outcomes for a stronger narrative of its activities and results, and, based on this, reinforcing its accountability system. These integrated reforms can help the CRU more effectively consolidate its role and responsibilities, match its resources to outputs, and communicate its performance to all stakeholders across government, industry and the public.

This report is part of the OECD work programme on the governance of regulators and regulatory policy, led by the OECD Network of Economic Regulators and the OECD Regulatory Policy Committee with the support of the Regulatory Policy Division of the OECD Directorate of Public Governance. The Directorate's mission is to help government at all levels design and implement strategic, evidence-based and innovative policies that support sustainable economic and social development.

Acknowledgements

This report was co-ordinated and prepared by Anna Pietikainen and Shelly Hsieh. The work underlying the report was led by Filippo Cavassini and Faisal Naru, with substantive inputs from Filippo Cavassini and Nick Malyshev, Head of the Regulatory Policy Division, and with the encouragement and support of Marcos Bonturi, Director, Public Governance Directorate. Special thanks go to Rolf Alter and Luiz de Mello, respectively Director and Deputy Director of the Public Governance Directorate when the review was launched and conducted for their support and inputs. Jennifer Stein co-ordinated the editorial process. Kate Lancaster and Andrea Uhrhammer provided editorial support.

The team included three peer reviewers from the members of the OECD Network of Economic Regulators (NER), who participated in a policy mission to Ireland and provided extensive inputs and feedback throughout the development of the review: Mr. Alberto Biancardi, Commissioner, Regulatory Authority for Electricity, Gas and Water (AEEGSI), Italy; Mr. Andrew Burgess, Associate Partner, Office of Gas and Electricity Markets (OFGEM), United Kingdom; and Mr. Carlos de Régules, Executive Director, Agency for Safety, Energy and Environment (ASEA), Mexico.

The report would not have been possible without the support of the Commission for Regulation of Utilities (CRU) and its staff. The team would in particular like to thank the following colleagues for their unique assistance in collecting data and information, organising the team's missions to Ireland and providing feedback at different stages of the development of the review: Paul McGowan, Chairperson; Garrett Blaney and Aoife MacEvilly, Commissioners; Laura Brien, Director of Energy Markets; Maeve Kennedy and Mairead Byrne, Personal Assistants. Ann McGarry, Director of Energy Safety; Sheenagh Rooney, Director of Water, Customer Care and Operations; and John Melvin, Director of Energy Networks and Legal also provided valuable inputs. Interviews and comments from various government, industry and public stakeholders during the review process also contributed to the analysis presented in the report.

A draft of the report was discussed at the OECD Network of Economic Regulators and presented to the OECD Regulatory Policy Committee in November 2017.

Table of contents

Foreword 3

Acknowledgements 5

Acronyms and abbreviations 9

Executive summary 11
Role and objectives 11
Input 12
Process 12
Output and outcome 13

Assessment and recommendations 15
Role and objectives 16
Input 24
Process 27
Output and outcome 33
Notes 38

Chapter 1. Regulatory and sector context 39
Institutions 43
Institutional and regulatory reform 43
References 47

Chapter 2. Governance of the Commission for Regulation of Utilities 49
Role and objectives 50
Input 66
Process 71
Output and outcome 78
Note 81
References 82

Annex A. Methodology 83
References 89

Tables

Table 1. Overview of CRU functions and regulated sectors 16
Table 2. CRU Strategic Goals 2014-18 21
Table 2.1. Main features of sectors regulated by the CRU 51
Table 2.2. Main Irish state-owned energy and water enterprises 52
Table 2.3. Co-ordination in gas and electricity sectors 59
Table 2.4. Co-ordination in energy safety 60

Table 2.5. Co-ordination in public water and waste water services 61
Table 2.6. Summary of changes to funding regulations 2015-17 66
Table 2.7. Annual operating budgets and expenditures at CRU 2015-17 (million EUR) 67
Table 2.8. Sanctions on staff headcount by DPER for 1 January to 31 December 2017 68
Table 2.9. Breakdown of CRU supporting and professional staff 68
Table 2.10. CRU professional workforce 69
Table 2.11. Breakdown of male and female employees according to staff categories (2016) 69
Table 2.12. CRU salary scales (EUR) before and after January 2016 70
Table 2.13. Appealing CRU Decisions 77
Table 2.14. Appealing SEM committee decisions 77
Table 2.15. CRU strategic goals and measures of success 2014-18 80

Table A A.1. Criteria for assessing regulators' own performance framework 86

Figures

Figure 1. Input-process output-outcome framework for performance indicators 37
Figure 2.1. Lead areas assigned to CRU Commissioners, as at October 2017 72
Figure 2.2. Internal structure of the CRU 73

Figure A A.1. The OECD Best Practice Principles on the Governance of Regulators 85
Figure A A.2. Input-process-output-outcome framework for performance indicators 87

Acronyms and abbreviations

ACER	Agency for the Cooperation of Energy Regulators
BGE	Bord Gáis Energy
CBA	Cost benefit analysis
CCPC	Competition and Consumer Protection Commission
CER	Commission for Energy Regulation
CRU	Commission for Regulation of Utilities
CSG	Consumer Stakeholder Group
DCCAE	Department of Communications, Climate Action and Environment
DfE	Department for the Economy (Northern Ireland)
DHPLG	Department of Housing, Planning, and Local Government
DPER	Department of Public Expenditure and Reform
DSO	Distribution System Operator
EPA	Environment Protection Agency
ERA	Electricity Regulation Act
ESB	Electricity Supply Board
ESBN	ESB Networks
GSF	Gas Safety Framework
HSA	Health and Safety Agency
IAA	Irish Aviation Authority
ICT	Information and Communication Technologies
IBP	Integrated Business Plan
IED	Industrial Emissions Directive (2010/75/EU)
IRCG	Irish Coast Guard
IPPC	Integrated pollution prevention and control
I-SEM	Integrated Single Electricity Market
JOC	Joint Oireachtas Committee
JSG	Joint Steering Group for the Single Electricity Market
KPI	Key performance indicator
LPG	Liquefied petroleum gas
MIC	Maximum import capacity
MSO	Marine survey office
MOU	Memorandum of understanding
NER	Network of Economic Regulators
NTMA	National Treasury Management Agency

OSCP	Oil spill contingency plan
PAFER	Performance assessment framework for economic regulators
PSF	Petroleum Safety Framework
PSO	Public Service Obligation
PWF	Public Water Forum
REFIT	Renewable energy feed-in-tariff
RGI	Registered gas installers
RIA	Regulatory Impact Assessment
SEM	Single Electricity Market
SEMC	SEM Committee
SEMO	Single Electricity Market Operator
SMP	System Marginal Price
SSB	Safety supervisor bodies
TAO	Transmission Asset Owner
TSO	Transmission system operator
UR	Northern Ireland Authority for Utility Regulation
WPAC	Water Policy Advisory Committee
WAREG	European Water Regulators

Executive summary

The Commission for Regulation of Utilities (CRU) is an independent multi-sector regulator with a range of economic, customer and safety functions and duties in Ireland's energy and water sectors. The CRU is a high-performing and well-regarded regulator that has, since its creation in 1999, successfully absorbed new functions and developed and implemented major policy reforms for the benefit of Irish consumers and the country's economy.

As the regulator continues to implement complex projects in a rapidly changing and uncertain policy context, its institutional and organisational capacity to operate effectively needs to be bolstered through integrated reforms to upgrade some of its external and internal governance functions, including strategic planning and human resource management mechanisms.

Role and objectives

The CRU is an independent regulator under the aegis of two Ministries (Department of Communications, Climate Action and Environment, DCCAE and Department of Housing, Planning and Local Government, DHPLG) and is governed by a series of sector-specific laws that have been amended over the years. Currently, the CRU is responsible for regulating energy markets, energy safety, and public water and wastewater services in Ireland. The CRU also shares cross-jurisdictional responsibilities for regulating the all-island Single Electricity Market (SEM), covering Ireland and Northern Ireland.

The CRU has built cordial and predictable ("no surprises") working relationships with the executive and other government entities. However, the gradual increase in the CRU's functions and the complex legal framework in which it operates make it difficult for both stakeholders and the regulator itself to fully understand the CRU's priorities. Moreover, while the regulator's activities are guided by five year Strategic Plans that focus on policy outcomes, it is not clear how these Plans are monitored or how they guide decision-making.

Key recommendations

- Assert the leadership of the CRU in setting its priorities as a multi-sector economic and safety regulator, using the next Strategic Plan (2019-2021) as an opportunity to do so; explore the possibility of setting up an advisory group that can act as sounding board for the definition of the Plan and annual work programmes.

- Strongly advocate for and contribute to the launch of a rationalisation of the CRU's legislative framework in the energy sector.

- Develop a comprehensive and well-resourced communications strategy that increases the transparency and predictability of informal information-sharing and co-ordination channels with the executive and the legislature.

Input

The CRU is independent in defining its budget and collecting its income. Generally, the regulator feels it is adequately resourced financially to fulfil its mandate and carry out its activities, and is able to manage financial resources autonomously.

In contrast, the CRU is constrained in the management of human resources by central government frameworks, leading to serious difficulties in attracting and retaining staff. In response to these challenges, the CRU has introduced ways to attract and retain staff, but reports that these are not sufficient.

Key recommendations

- Use the Strategic Plan of the CRU as the guiding framework for all planning and monitoring activities, including developing a multi-year human and financial resource framework.

- Take full advantage of the opportunity to present a business case for the review of overall CRU staff levels with the DCCAE and the DHPLG, as appropriate, following regular workforce planning exercises.

- Join with other Irish economic regulators to advocate and make the case for taking into account the "special needs" of economic regulators in Irish public administration practices.

Process

Decision-making and information-sharing processes at the CRU are fluid and effective and have been further improved with recently introduced internal planning and management tools.

As an independent regulator, the CRU is accountable to the Oireachtas and prepares annual reports for this purpose, but the regulator's activities and results are not addressed in formal dialogue channels.

In addition, the CRU engages with stakeholders systematically and transparently in its regulatory activities. This engagement could be complemented by other tools of good regulatory practice.

Key recommendations

- Instate structured mechanisms for the presentation of CRU annual reports to Oireachtas standing committees, including for activities of the SEM Committee.

- Take the lead on the uptake of good regulatory practices (impact assessment, *ex post* evaluation, stakeholder engagement) in a proportional and targeted manner, and use these practices to foment internal learning as well as promote the better regulation agenda within the Irish government.

- Continue to actively engage with consumers through dedicated forums, in addition to available channels for online stakeholder consultation.

Output and outcome

CRU activities are guided by multi-year Strategic Plans that focus on policy outcomes, but it is not clear how these Plans are monitored or guide decision-making. The Strategic Plan is operationalised through annual work programmes with comprehensive indicators, but the strategic and operational plans are not fully aligned. Moreover, the CRU has the power to request and collect a large amount of information from regulated energy entities.

Key recommendations

- Use the Strategic Plan as a tool for reporting on CRU performance and results, and seize the opportunity to use the 2019-21 Strategic Plan to develop this comprehensive and streamlined performance assessment and reporting framework.

- In the new framework, align goals and indicators between the Strategic Plan and annual work programmes, for easier monitoring and reporting, using simplified performance indicators that focus on measurable deliverables.

- Ensure the collection of appropriate data from regulated entities to inform CRU reporting and analytical activities.

Assessment and recommendations

Since its creation in 1999, the Commission for Regulation of Utilities (CRU) has successfully developed and implemented major policy reforms for the benefit of Irish consumers and the country's economy.[1] As a result, for example, it currently oversees fully competitive electricity and gas markets in Ireland as well as an all-island single electricity market with the Utility Regulator in Northern Ireland. The regulator has helped achieve these policy goals while building cordial relationships and effective co-ordination and communication mechanisms with sector stakeholders. The CRU is acknowledged across government, parliament and industry as a technically capable and professional regulator, a reputation that it enjoys both at domestic and EU level. The regulator has also implemented actions to improve its internal management processes in line with best practice; some of these are on-going.

As the regulator continues to lead on the implementation of complex projects in a rapidly changing, uncertain and highly political context, its institutional and organisational capacity to operate effectively needs to be bolstered through an upgrade of some of its external and internal governance functions, including strategic planning and human resources management mechanisms. The delivery of complex policy objectives (water regulation, smart meters, and cross-border power markets) in rapidly transforming energy and water sectors calls for bolstered processes and legitimacy. This should start with the identification of priorities, their communication as well as the consolidation of the regulator's *de facto* independence, that could be supported by a wider effort towards better understanding of *de jure* and *de facto* independence within the context of the Irish government. This stronger institutional identity could help the CRU fill a gap in its autonomy with regard to attracting and retaining human resources, which is likely to become a greater challenge as the economy recovers. It would also complement the financial autonomy the CRU already enjoys. In this context, the regulator can use its upcoming three-year Strategic Plan exercise as a guiding framework for setting its priorities and creating a stronger accountability and resources-to-results framework, which would include setting up a more structured and predictable relationship with Parliament. In addition, building on its reputation as economic and safety regulator, the CRU could use this opportunity to bolster its processes and practices to aim high with regard to the proportional and targeted use of good regulatory practices. This could provide the basis for contributing to the advancement of the Better Regulation agenda in Ireland, and build alliances with other economic regulators.

These changes and reforms are not "nice to have" improvements. Rather, they should be seen as a comprehensive and necessary reform package that will enable the regulator to enhance its performance, stand up to future scrutiny and ensure that the multiple challenges it faces are adequately addressed.

Role and objectives

The CRU is an independent multi-sector regulator with a range of economic, customer and safety functions and duties that have gradually increased over the years. Since the creation of the agency in 1999, its sectoral responsibilities have been gradually expanded from the electricity sector to encompass gas (2002), energy safety (2006) and economic regulation of water (2013). The decisions to broaden the CRU's areas of responsibility have been motivated by a positive assessment of its regulatory performance and its capacity to absorb functions in new policy areas, as well as in response to energy regulatory obligations of European legislation. The CRU currently holds a variety of functions across sectors that are at different stages of development and maturity, several of which feature state-owned companies (Table 1).

Table 1. Overview of CRU functions and regulated sectors

Sector	CRU function	Market structure
Electricity (since 1999)	• Grant licences for electricity generation and supply, transmission system operation, and transmission and distribution asset ownership licence • Authorise construction of generation stations • Provide access to electricity transmission and distribution systems • Monitor and regulate competitive wholesale and retail markets • Oversee rights and obligations of electricity undertakings in the all-island Single Electricity Market (SEM) • Regulate revenues that can be recovered by network companies • Calculate and certify annual Public Service Obligation (PSO) levy for generation from sustainable, renewable and indigenous sources • Inspect, review and collect information from regulated entities • Advise the Minister on electricity generation and on the exercise of ministerial functions under the relevant legislation	• Full market opening (competition) in 2005 • Single Electricity Market established in 2007 • Prices in business market segments deregulated 2010 • Prices in domestic market segment deregulated 2011 • State-owned companies currently active: ESB (including subsidiary Electric Ireland), ESB Networks, EirGrid, Bord na Móna
Gas (since 2002)	• Grant licences to ship and supply natural gas, and gas transmission and distribution asset ownership and operation • Provide access to gas transmission and distribution systems • Monitor and regulate competitive development of gas supply • Monitor and regulate competitive gas retail market • Set tariffs for gas transmission and distribution operated by Gas Networks Ireland • Regulate revenues that can be recovered by Gas Networks Ireland • Inspect, review and collect information from regulated entities	• Full market opening (competition) in 2007 • Prices in business market segments deregulated 2011 • Domestic market (Bord Gáis Energy) prices deregulated 2014 • State-owned companies currently active: Ervia/Gas Networks Ireland (GNI), ESB/Electric Ireland – gas retail supplier

Sector	CRU function	Market structure
Energy safety (since 2006)	• Regulate gas network safety including transmission and distribution systems • Regulate petroleum (oil and gas) safety, including exploration, extraction and decommissioning (onshore and offshore) safety • Design and oversee safety supervisory schemes for electrical contractors and natural gas & LPG installers • Set programme of audit and inspection of regulated entities • Issue safety permits for petroleum activities and safety licences to LPG undertakings Promotion and public awareness of electrical and gas safety issues	• Currently 2 sets of petroleum safety permit holders: the Kinsale Gas Fields (decommissioning in 3 years) and the Corrib Gas Field (incipient) • 23 natural gas and LPG undertakings have presented safety cases to the CRU as at March 2017 • 2971 registered gas installers and 4213 registered electrical contractors in Dec 2016
Water (since 2013)	• Regulate the economic provision of water services by Irish water • Advise the Minister on water policy and service developments • Specify minimum standards of service by Irish Water • Protect the interests of water consumers • Approve, reject or modify codes of practice on standards of performance by Irish Water • Direct Irish Water to comply with approved code of practice • Provide dispute resolution service to customers of Irish Water	• Prior to 2013, 34 local water bodies in 26 counties • National water utility company Irish Water established 2013 • Start of residential water metering program 2013 • Residential water tariffs introduced 2015 • Residential water tariffs and metering program suspended 2016 • Expert Commission and Oireachtas review on water funding issues and metering, recommendations 2017 • State-owned companies currently active: Irish Water

The CRU is governed by a series of sector-specific laws that have been amended over the years in response to sector evolutions and EU directives, resulting in a complex and at times fragmented legislative landscape. The CRU's objectives and functions are defined in three legislative texts for the electricity sector, one for gas, four for energy safety and four for water.[2] The existence of parallel legislative texts that have been modified repeatedly over the years (26 times in the case of the Electricity Regulation Act of 1999) are seen to stand in the way of a clear understanding of the CRU's objectives and their order of priority. As of the end of 2017, the Department of Communications, Climate Action and Environment (DCCAE) has already committed to a review of the legal and institutional framework for the regulation of electricity and natural gas markets, including the CRU's mandate and resourcing.

The gradual increase in the CRU's sectors of responsibility and functions as well as the complex legal framework complicate or even obfuscate understanding of the CRU's priorities by stakeholders and the regulator itself. The CRU's areas of responsibility in the energy sector have increased over the years, creating potential confusion and conflict in certain areas over priorities. For instance, the CRU is responsible for promoting new businesses by issuing licences for gas and electricity undertakings, and at same time, regulating safety in the same sectors. Noting this potential conflict of interest, the ALARP ("as low as reasonably practicable") Guidance Part of the Petroleum Safety Framework and the Gas Safety Regulatory Framework, measures). In cases where the outcome of such an assessment is inconclusive, the ALARP guidance requires the application of a Precautionary Principle is applied to assessment decisions, whereby "safety is expected to take precedence over economic considerations" and that "in this decision context, the decision could have significant economic consequences to an organisation in conjunction with the safety implications" (ALARP 2016, 18). Additionally, since 2013, the regulator has been operating as a multi-sector economic and technical regulator. These changes in the regulator's mandate are made more complex by the rapid transformation of the energy sector, large investments needs in a highly politicised water sector and uncertainties following Brexit. In addition to reviewing the legislative framework for electricity and gas regulation, there is need for more assertive setting and public communication of priorities, including any trade-offs, by the regulator.

The CRU is an independent regulator under the aegis of two Departments that are responsible for setting policy that guides the regulator's activities. The CRU operates under the aegis of the DCCAE for its energy (including energy safety) functions and, since 2013, the Department of Housing, Planning and Local Government (DHPLG) for the economic regulation of water. The two Departments are responsible for setting sectoral policies that frame CRU operations. The CRU formally provides annual work plans to the two Ministers and annual reports to the Oireachtas, the Irish Parliament, via the DCCAE who lays it before the Oireachtas. This channel of communication reflects the requirements of the legislation for the communication of such documents to the Oireachtas rather than any formal approval or appraisal of the documents by the Departments. The existence of two parallel channels of communication (via two Departments) to other parts of the Irish public administration since 2013 occasionally results in duplicated work for the CRU, in particular with respect to resource management.

The CRU shares cross-jurisdictional responsibilities for regulating the all-island Single Electricity Market (SEM), covering Ireland and Northern Ireland, and is in progress to link up with EU countries in an Integrated Single Electricity Market (I-SEM), raising questions for the future of the market in the context of Brexit. The SEM/I-SEM is regulated by the SEM Committee (SEMC), which comprises representatives from the CRU and Utility Regulator (UR) of Northern Ireland, along with independent members. In response to recent European legislation to create a single wholesale electricity market across Europe, the SEMC is currently working to redesign the SEM to facilitate coupling with the electricity market in the rest of Europe. The future evolution of the regulatory governance of I-SEM and its alignment with the European market will need to take into account the impact of the United Kingdom leaving the EU.

As economic regulator the CRU has successfully delivered the deregulation of Ireland's retail electricity and gas markets. Electricity and gas retail markets have been fully deregulated between 2005 and 2014 and the CRU no longer regulates prices in these sectors. Regarding electricity networks, the CRU regulates the level of revenue which the monopoly electricity Transmission System Operator (TSO) (EirGrid), the monopoly Transmission Asset Owner (TAO) (ESB Networks) in Ireland and the monopoly electricity Distribution System Operator (DSO) (ESB Networks) can recover. In gas the CRU regulates the level of revenue which Gas Networks Ireland (GNI), the gas Transmission System Operator (TSO) and gas Distribution System Operator (DSO) can recover. Electricity Transmission and Distribution revenues are set by the CRU and reviewed every five years. These revenues are collected by the TSO and DSO from charges to energy suppliers using the networks, who may in turn choose to pass on the costs to their customers. Gas Transmission and Distribution revenues are set in the same manner as electricity network revenues.

The reform of the provision of water services is an ongoing challenge for the government and a highly politicised issue in Ireland. Attempts to improve the efficiency of water service delivery by consolidating 34 local water service providers into a single water services authority, Irish Water, and introduce domestic water charges have been heavily scrutinised by the media and public. At present, the costs of providing domestic water services continue to be funded by the government and regulated by the CRU. Current legislation provides that the CRU has authority to review and approve or refuse to approve Irish Water's "water charges plan" in light of its analysis of Irish Water's investment plan and other costs.

The CRU carries out different types of inspections and has a range of safety enforcement powers. The CRU carries out annual Audits of licenced electricity and gas Suppliers to monitor compliance with the Supplier Handbook; the most recently published audit report was the 2016 CRU Audit of Compliance with the Code of Practice on Vulnerable Customers. The regulator has recently been granted sanctioning powers to fine regulated entities in case of non-compliance, but how these powers will be used is currently being defined. Up to now, the CRU can only address non-compliance through notices or, in the most extreme case, licence revocation. With regard to the CRU's energy safety functions, the CRU defines an audit and inspection programme in its annual work programme, where topics to be reviewed are decided upon by taking into account previous audit and inspection findings, incident reports and safety case risk ratings. Where a regulated entity does not sufficiently address identified issues or non-compliance within set and agreed timelines, the CRU can take enforcement action; the regulator can also skip straight to enforcement where considered proportionate The CRU expects its inspection and compliance related activities to increase in the near future. Inspection reports and recommendations in energy safety are not made public.

The CRU enjoys a cordial and predictable ("no surprises") working relationship with the executive and other government entities designed to contribute to more effective policymaking by the Irish public administration. The CRU is one of several economic regulators under the aegis of the DCCAE and the only economic regulator under the DHPLG. While the relationship with DHPLG is new and currently being defined in legislation and the relationship with DCCAE is of longer-standing, the CRU's collaboration with both parent Departments is considered productive and cordial by all parties. The CRU provides both informal and formal inputs to the DCCAE and DHPLG on policy formulation and advises the Minister. CRU senior management meets with Ministers or senior management in the respective Departments on a regular basis to discuss activities and sector evolutions for the purposes of information sharing. In some instances, such as when providing feedback to EU legislation, DCCAE relies on CRU technical expertise. In the water sector, DHPLG has called on the CRU frequently to provide advice on matters pertaining to CRU duties. Given the size of the administration, personal connections between staff of CRU, DCCAE and DHPLG are prevalent and are seen to aid effective communications. Co-ordination with other government entities, such as the Environmental Protection Agency (EPA), generally appears fluid and constructive.

Government counterparts and regulated entities have a positive assessment of the CRU's capacities and its technical work, but the regulator and its work seem to be less well known by the legislature and the general public. Stakeholders in government and regulated entities present an overall positive assessment of their relationship with the

CRU as well as the work of the regulator. On the other hand, the highly technical nature of the regulator's work and the absence of outreach in plain language to non-specialists to explain the CRU's activities and decisions undermine general understanding of the CRU's role, functions, the results of its work and its independence. More, better targeted and less technical outreach would bolster not only the CRU's positioning with the general public but could also add value to its relations with the Oireachtas. More accessible information on the CRU's role, independence and technical merit could be accompanied with carefully designed communication campaigns on topics such as the continued reform of water charges or the introduction of smart meters to contribute to smoother implementation. A major campaign to communicate its role and responsibilities to the public is planned when the name change of the regulator from the Commission for Energy Regulation (CER) to the Commission for the Regulation of Utilities (CRU) is made effective (October 2017); the recent appointment of a communications manager at the CRU also supports this goal.

CRU activities are guided by multi-year Strategic Plans that focus on policy outcomes, but it is not clear how these Plans are monitored or guide decision-making. The CRU's current Strategic Plan refers to the 2014-18 period and proposes six Strategic goals for this period (Table 2 below). Five of the six goals focus appropriately on the policy outcomes of the CRU's mandate, serving as a compass for the CRU's activities during this period, with one out of six goals referring to management of resources and the quality of regulatory processes. The plan attaches measures of success and implementation strategies for each goal, as well as a provision for a regular revision of the goals in rapidly evolving sectoral contexts, but it is not clear how monitoring or reviews are carried out or how they may influence decision-making. The Strategic Plan will cover three years (2019-21) for the next planning period.

The regulator's annual priorities are expressed in yearly work programmes, but linkages between the Strategic Plan and annual priorities could be further strengthened. The CRU has begun developing annual Integrated Business Plans (IBP) to provide clear linkages between strategy, risk, resources, work plans and reporting procedures to improve project management outcomes. The CRU is also in progress to create linkages between its medium-term strategy planning with annual and quarterly work planning and reporting. However, there are still important gaps to be bridged; for example, the objectives of the IBP do not currently follow the structure of the six strategic goals, and indicators do not link back to the measures of success defined in the Strategic Plan, making it difficult to align and track a consistent progress between the two plans. This may lead to duplication of effort and inefficient monitoring, evaluation and reporting of outcomes, and learnings.

Table 2. CRU Strategic Goals 2014-18

Goal 1	TO ENSURE THAT "energy and gas are supplied safely" **A WORLD CLASS PUBLIC SAFETY RECORD**
Goal 2	TO ENSURE THAT "the lights stay on" **SECURE ELECTRICITY SUPPLIES FROM PRODUCTION TO CONSUMPTION**
Goal 3	TO ENSURE THAT "the gas continues to flow" **SECURE NATURAL GAS SUPPLIES WITH IMPROVED DIVERSITY OF SOURCES**
Goal 4	TO ENSURE "a reliable supply of clean water and efficient treatment of wastewater" **SECURE, ROBUST WATER SUPPLIES AND WASTE WATER DISPOSAL**
Goal 5	TO ENSURE THAT "the prices charged are fair and reasonable" **FULLY COMPETITIVE RETAIL MARKETS AND WELL-REGULATED NETWORKS,DELIVERING FAIR AND EFFICIENT PRICES TO CUSTOMERS**
Goal 6	TO ENSURE "regulation is best international practice" **LIVING UP TO OUR VALUES**

Source: CER (2013); "Strategic Plan 2014-18: Regulating Water, Energy and Energy Safety in the Public Interest", Commission for Energy Regulation, Dublin.

Recommendations

- ***Assert the leadership of the CRU in setting its priorities as a multi-sector economic and safety regulator.*** Building this stronger institutional identity should start with the identification of priorities, their communication as well as the consolidation of the CRU's de facto independence. This effort could also build on a greater and more widely shared understanding of the CRU's de jure and de facto independence. The CRU can embrace the opportunity provided by the definition of its 2019-21 Strategic Plan to lead a consultative and open process to define and communicate its priorities, including any trade-offs, consolidating its de facto independence into its strategic planning exercise.

- ***Set up the next Strategic Plan (2019-21) as the guiding framework for all of the regulator's planning, resourcing, prioritisation, monitoring and reporting activities.*** To fulfil this role the Plan will need to include a clear baseline and monitoring and reporting arrangements of targets that can then be further broken down in annual work plans including data on estimated financial and human resources required for implementation. Aligning annual work plans and reporting and results (including performance indicators) to the widely consulted and agreed Strategic Plan would make planning, monitoring and reporting more efficient, would create a more coherent storyline for the CRU's communications around its results and impact and finally, would contribute to a better understanding of the linkages between the CRU's human resources and its ability to deliver results. The Plan should also be costed and operationalised by more detailed costed annual integrated business plans over time.

- ***Strongly advocate for the rationalisation of the CRU's legislative framework in the energy sector and contribute to any process initiated for that purpose.*** A careful review and reform of the legislative texts that govern CRU objectives and functions would support a stronger identity and clearer priorities for the regulator and stakeholders at large. This rationalisation of energy legislation is an important objective of the CRU.

Box 1. Corporate strategy and annual forward work programme of OFGEM in the United Kingdom

In light of its statutory duties, OFGEM has developed a corporate strategy that sets out, amongst other things, OFGEM's mission, outcomes, regulatory approaches, priority activities (OFGEM, 2014). OFGEM has also separately published regulatory stances, which are principles which it had regard to in developing policy within the limits of its statutory duties (OFGEM, 2016a). These regulatory stances are:

- Promoting effective competition to deliver for consumers
- Driving value in monopoly activities through competition and incentive regulation
- Supporting innovation in technologies, systems and business models
- Managing risk for efficient and sustainable energy
- Protecting the interests of consumers in vulnerable situations

In the context of its corporate strategy, OFGEM establishes an annual forward work programme. OFGEM initially publishes a draft forward work programme, and then seeks submissions on this work programme, which then considers finalising the forward work programme (for example, OFGEM's draft Forward Work Program for 2017-18 was released for consultation on 19 December 2016, with submissions due on 15 February 2017, and the final work program due to be released in March 2017 (OFGEM, 2016b).

The draft forward work programme for 2017-18 sets out key initiatives, within which the draft forward work programme identifies specific pieces of work that OFGEM considers will deliver the greatest benefit to consumers given its resources. The initiatives in OFGEM's draft forward work programme for 2017-18 are (OFGEM, 2016b):

- Enabling a better functioning retail market
- Facilitating the energy transition
- Learning from the first RIIO framework and setting RIIO-2 up for success
- Introducing competition in monopoly areas
- Becoming an authoritative source of quality analysis

The forward work programme also sets out OFGEM's budget for the period, and includes regulatory and e-serve performance indicators and deliverables for each of the pieces of work under the initiatives.

Source: OFGEM (2014), "Our Strategy", https://www.ofgem.gov.uk/sites/default/files/docs/2014/12/corporate_strategy_0.pdf (accessed 4 April 2017), OFGEM (2016a), "OFGEM's regulatory stances", https://www.ofgem.gov.uk/publications-and-updates/ofgems-regulatory-stances (accessed 4 April 2017), OFGEM (2016b), "Forward Work Programme 2017-18", https://www.ofgem.gov.uk/system/files/docs/2016/12/draft_forward_work_programme_2017-18.pdf (accessed 4 April 2017).

- ***Build more transparency into some of the informal information-sharing and co-ordination channels with the executive and the legislature.*** It is positive that there is fluid communication between the CRU, Departments and the Oireachtas. However, whenever possible and appropriate, there would be merit in communicating more proactively on meetings with the Department or the Joint Oireachtas Committees, for example, on issues concerning long-term trends and challenges in the sectors overseen by the CRU. This could include communicating that a high-level meeting with the Department or the Joint Oireachtas Committee has occurred and topics that were discussed, via enhanced CRU communication channels and social media. This would contribute to inform stakeholders and enhance CRU overall accountability framework and identity as independent regulator.

- ***Design, resource and implement a comprehensive communications strategy for the CRU.*** This communications and outreach strategy would seek to build in strategic communications into all of the regulator's activities and would aim to increase understanding of the CRU's role and functions, the results of its work as well as provide information on upcoming decisions and how they will impact consumers and markets. The communications strategy should (internally) define objectives, activities and means for different target audiences (general public, the Oireachtas, the media, other relevant stakeholders within and outside government), taking particularly into account outreach to consumers and non-specialists. It should also include potential impacts on the all island single electricity market in the context of the Brexit. The change of the name of the Commission from the Commission for Energy Regulation (CER) to the Commission for Regulation of Utilities (CRU) in October 2017 offers a good opportunity to re-position the CRU's communications activities.

- ***Assess if any mechanisms or duties of the CRU could be outsourced to third party providers, with the CRU maintaining responsibility for quality and oversight.*** For areas that could be outsourced, a register of pre-approved third parties could be set up to facilitate contracting. The exercise may also lead to the identification of duties or mechanisms that are obsolete or could be automated, and could further alleviate CRU workload.

- ***Continue developing a risk-based approach to enforcement across all regulated sectors.*** The OECD Best Practice Principles for Regulatory Policy on Regulatory Enforcement and Inspections (2014) propose as their third principle risk-focus and proportionality, whereby the frequency of inspections and the resources employed should be proportional to the level of risk and enforcement actions should be aiming at reducing the actual risk posed by infractions. Although this is already the practice concerning safety case for offshore operations, it could be applied virtually to all inspection related activities.

- ***Pilot joint safety risk assessments inspections with other regulators.*** This would alleviate the burden on the regulated sector and activate synergies with other regulators in the energy and water sectors (e.g. EPA).

Input

The CRU is independent in defining its budget and collecting its income. The CRU is entirely funded through levies and licence fees from regulated entities (although indirectly, levy income from Irish Water is provided for from government budget). Levies from market participants constitute the bulk of income and are defined annually on a cost-recovery basis in the 4th quarter of the year, on the basis of an estimate of CRU operating and capital budget required for the next year. The Commissioners review the proposals and formally approve the budget by 30 November of each year, and the CRU Finance team prepares and publishes all statutory instruments to enact levy orders in a timely fashion. In accordance with the regulator's independence as provided in legislation, the CRU's budget or levies are not reviewed or approved by the executive or legislative branches of government. The CRU collects the levies directly, which do not go through the government budget.

Sources of funding are linked directly to expenditures in the CRU budget by sector, and the multi-sector model of the regulator allows for sharing costs for certain central functions. Direct costs in the CRU budget are attributed to regulated sectors, as is staff time as per time allocated to delivery of core activities. Shared costs as well as staff time spent on horizontal or administrative functions (finance, HR, communications, etc.) are allocated transparently to each sector as per the projected headcount engaged in the relevant sectors. In 2017, expenditure per sector as percentage of overall expenditure was as follows: electricity 57%, gas 20%, energy safety 8% and water 15%.

Generally the regulator feels it is adequately resourced financially to fulfil its mandate and carry out its activities, and is able to manage financial resources autonomously. Operating on a cost-recovery basis, the CRU is able to raise sufficient funds for its activities. Over the years, increase in responsibilities has been accompanied by a proportional increase in financial resources. Moreover, based on a risk assessment, a contingency fund is defined on a yearly basis to provide flexibility to deal with potential legal challenges or costs linked to safety cases or events. Any excess of revenue in the financial year is taken into account in determining the levy for the subsequent year per sector. The CRU can carry unspent funds over to the following year's budget without review or approval from external government entities. This gives the CRU a strong basis to act independently.

In contrast to its autonomous funding and financial management model, the CRU is constrained in the management of human resources by central government frameworks, leading to difficulties in attracting and retaining staff. The CRU is subject to caps on its headcount from the Department of Expenditure and Public Reform (DPER), as per the government Employee Control Framework (ECF), introduced as part of the public sector reforms following the financial crisis and in keeping with the central government requirement to monitor and control public sector staffing, payments and liabilities. An ECF letter is used by the parent Department(s) at the beginning of each year to confirm headcount for the coming year. Typically, the CRU would advocate for additional headcount with its parent Departments and by extension DPER when it takes on a new function, and generally has not sought to increase headcount outside of these occasions. Since 2016, the headcount has been set at 105. This is generally felt to correspond to the workload of the regulator. A greater challenge is created by the application of government salary scales and inflexible terms and conditions of hire, particularly the requirement to appoint new staff at the lowest point of each pay grade, and that are generally not competitive with the private sector. The CRU is able to assign positions flexibly within the agreed salary scales for each grade, but recruitment for the highest grades requires the presentation of a business case by the parent Department(s) to DPER, as part of the overall envelope under the jurisdiction of the parent Department (i.e. the parent Department may be obliged to make trade-offs between different entities that it oversees). This poses challenges to staff recruitment and retention, and may hinder the delivery of CRU outputs. This issue is more pronounced at the analyst level than at the senior levels, as CRU staff who have accumulated two or three years of regulatory experience become highly valuable to industry that are in a position to offer more competitive salaries. Moreover, lack of flexibility to hire temporary staff to work on emerging issues or during peaks is flagged as an issue.

In response to these challenges, the CRU has introduced ways to attract and retain staff, but reports that this is not sufficient. Recently, since mid-2016 and following a negotiation with DPER, the CRU has introduced two separate salary levels for analyst positions which allow it to recruit more senior analysts directly (previously all analysts had to start at the lowest level unless otherwise agreed with DPER through the parent Department). Moreover, the CRU offers a number of training and development opportunities for its staff, including running a graduate programme and funding educational assistance programmes to provide non-financial incentives to retain key members of staff. However, it is still reported that once more junior staff have built up their competences, they are likely to migrate to the private sector and that the CRU is unable to attract staff over from regulated entities or other organisations at appropriate levels of experience, which seems to be one the greatest challenge faced by the CRU. There is a risk that the CRU might face even greater challenges in attracting and retaining staff as Ireland's economy and labour market continues to improve.

In addition, the CRU has implemented strategies to deal with lack of headcount or specialists by resorting to consultancy contracts to support its work at times of higher workload. The CRU is not subject to constraints with regard to external consultancies and it has been able to rely on external support for highly technical work or in case of temporary heightened work load. While the use of consultants may be preferable in the aforementioned cases, in other cases the reliance on support from temporary staff may pose problems with regard to institutional memory as well as the reputation of the regulator and the opportunity to receive unbiased and objective advice, for example, when external consultants have been leading work engaging with regulated entities.

The CRU has developed solid IT systems for external and internal data collection functions that make for effective data management practices. Externally, stakeholders when required submit data to the regulator via online platforms and reports are generated automatically for the regulator. Internally, the Integrated Business Plan is reported on a quarterly basis via an IT platform by Divisions, and monitoring reports are automatically compiled for review by the Commissioners.

Recommendations

- *Use the Strategic Plan of the CRU as the guiding framework for all of the regulator's planning and monitoring activities, including the production a multi-year human and financial resource framework.* Costing the three-year Strategic Plan will provide longer-term visibility to the CRU regarding its financial needs and the levy structure of the sectors it regulates. The first year of the three-year Plan would be translated into a more detailed budget attached to the Annual Integrated Business Plan.

- *Take full advantage of the opportunity to present a business case for the review of overall CRU headcount with parent Departments, as appropriate, following regular work force planning exercises.* On foot of the three-year Strategic Plan, the CRU should approach is two parent Departments as part of one process with regard to workforce plans and staffing needs, and request that they also present their CRU case to DPER as one package, reflecting the complexity of the regulator's multi-sector responsibilities to DPER.

- *Ally with other Irish economic regulators to advocate and make the case for the "special needs" of economic regulators in the landscape of the Irish public administration and its practices.* Addressing the common challenges faced by economic regulators jointly – rather than in competition – will give more strength and credibility to messages and requests. This would include:

  o advocating for greater flexibility on salary and employment grades and the use of temporary staff;

  o exploring the introduction / maintenance of allowances or performance related pay;

  o setting up a joint graduate scheme (that could operate outside of the headcount sanction provided by DPER) and staff exchange programmes, contributing to creating a profession and culture of staff at economic regulators across the country.

Box 2. The establishment of an integrated system of energy regulators in Mexico

The recent energy reform that opened the oil and gas sector to private investment in Mexico in 2013 enhanced the institutional set-up of the existing economic regulators: the upstream regulator, the National Commission for Hydrocarbons (*Comisión Nacional de Hidrocarburos*, CNH) and the downstream regulator, the Commission for Energy Regulation (*Comisión Reguladora de Energía*, CRE). The reform also created a new cross-cutting technical regulator to oversee safety and environmental protection throughout the whole hydrocarbon value chain: the Agency for Safety, Energy and Environment (*Agencia de Seguridad, Energía y Ambiente*, ASEA).

Recently the three regulators have come together and formalised a Cooperation Agreement and a joint working group (GRUVI) around four main objectives:

1. Planning: to share a common vision of the future and plan accordingly
2. Operational co-ordination: to address operating priorities in a timely manner
3. Resources: to address common necessities concerning talent attraction and retention and financial autonomy
4. Conflict resolution: to address and resolve conflicts between regulators

---

Although quite recent, the GRUVI will begin yielding results shortly: the three planning divisions are sharing their independent planning exercises and are preparing to hold a joint planning session for the 2018-22 business plans ; on an operational level ASEA has been responding to both CNH and CRE operational demands as they emerge as a result of new operators entering the downstream market and the management of the newly signed contracts between new upstream operators and the State; a first round of temporary inter regulators technical staff exchange (internship programme) will commence by the Q4 of 2017.

Also the GRUVI has proven to be a good mechanism for putting together a package of statutory and legal proposals that aim at bolstering the integrated system of regulators institutional set-up and independence. These proposals are being jointly discussed with relevant government stakeholders.

Source: Information provided by ASEA, 2017.

- ***Continue to explore and propose solutions making the CRU a more attractive employer, from flexibility within the government salary scale to non-financial rewards and career development opportunities.*** The CRU could monitor salary and other benefit gaps with the regulated sector for comparable positions and seek to adapt its salary and benefit scale to minimise any gaps. This would help ensure the CRU has the right quality, skills and experience to challenge the industries it regulates and deliver benefits for consumers. It could also help target training and development opportunities for different positions. The CRU should continue to advocate for greater flexibility in setting salary scales within the regulator to be able to compete with the regulated sector in attracting and retaining staff, and further develop the offer of training and development opportunities for staff. This should be based on a "total rewards" approach, which takes into consideration not only financial incentives but also non-financial incentives to attract and retain staff, including considering the satisfaction of participating in a highly valued work culture and career development opportunities within the economic regulation area.

Process

Decision-making and governing body

The CRU is headed by a Commission that acts as an executive Board, participating in regulatory as well as managerial decision-making. The three-person Commission is responsible for setting the strategic direction for the CRU, monitoring its performance, and ensuring CRU's compliance with the law as well as the organisation's constitution and policies. Commissioners are appointed by the Minister, usually but not always following a competitive procedure with transparent job descriptions including specific selection criteria published. Neither the process nor profile requirements are made explicit in law. Commissioners' terms are prescribed in legislation (Electricity Regulation Act, 1999) as being no less than five and not more than seven years. Their mandates can be renewed once, for a total maximum number of years of ten. Commissioners' terms are staggered so that no more than one vacancy should arise in any one twelve month period. The Chair of the Commission is selected by the Minister from the serving Commissioners on a rotating basis for a period of typically two to three years, but this is not prescribed.

According to the Electricity Regulation Act (1999, Section 8.5), a member of the Commission may be removed by the Minister if deemed incapable through ill-health of effectively performing his or her duties or for stated misbehaviour.

Decision-making and information-sharing between the Commission and CRU senior management appear fluid and effective. The functioning of the Commission is clearly set out in its Rules and Procedures, and the Commissioners come together once a week in meetings that also include the CRU's four directors and, where necessary, managers or other relevant staff. In the current composition of the Commission, decisions are made on a consensual basis and have not been put to a vote. Each Commissioner has lead responsibility for specific technical and managerial areas; these areas of responsibility rotate between the Commissioners ensuring a high level of engagement in the quality of decisions. Commissioners delegate authority to Directors as appropriate for technical decision-making. Higher level policy decisions and priority setting should remain the remit of the Commissioners.

Transparency and accountability

While formally the Commission is accountable to parliament, structured reporting mechanisms are weak. The Commissioners are accountable to the Oireachtas and annual reports are sent to the DCCAE, for onward submission to the Oireachtas, but there is no systematic forum for their presentation or discussion. The CRU can be called to appear to answer specific questions on an ad hoc basis by the two standing committees that it reports to – the Committee on Communications, Climate Change and Natural Resources, and the Committee on Housing, Planning, and Local Government. The Committees feel they lack in-depth technical understanding of the work of the CRU and, in addition to more structured dialogue, would welcome more opportunities to become more familiar with the CRU as the regulator has already been doing via proactive meetings with members of parliament.

The cross-jurisdictional nature of the all-island Single Electricity Market (SEM) means that there are multiple accountability mechanisms for the SEM Committee (SEMC). In light of the on-going Brexit process, it will be particularly important to regularly inform the respective jurisdictions on impacts and proposed changes to the all island single electricity market. The SEMC regulates the single electricity market and is composed of the three CRU Commissioners, three UR representatives as well as an independent member and a deputy independent member. Regulators may individually or jointly appear before relevant bodies responsible for oversight in either jurisdiction (Northern Ireland or Ireland) to address all-island matters. While there is no singular cross-jurisdictional accountability mechanism for the SEM, an All-Island Joint Steering Group provides an oversight function for the SEMC as well as helps facilitate policy consistency and implementation of SEMC decisions. The SEMC has undertaken RIA for major policy changes but a more systematic and targeted use of RIA for high-impact decisions would enhance the effectiveness of regulatory decisions and highlight potential impacts on the all island single market. This will become increasingly important as the SEM integrates into the broader European electricity market.

The CRU's accountability framework is governed by government wide legislation and audit procedures. The CRU is governed by the Code of Practice for the Governance of State Bodies, most recently updated in 2016. The Code covers areas such as the Roles, Effectiveness and Codes of Conduct for the Board, Chairperson and Board Members; Business and financial reporting requirements; Guidance for Audit and Risk Committees;

Relations with the Oireachtas, Minister and parent Departments; Remuneration, Superannuation, and Official Entitlements; and Customer Service Quality. How the updated Code would be applied to independent regulators such as the CRU is currently being defined by parent departments and being progressed by the CRU for compliance by the end of its financial year (31 December 2017). Moreover, CRU senior management and staff are held to account by other existing government-wide legislation such as the Ethics in Public Office Acts of 1995 and 2001, The CRU also has its own additional Code of conduct that sets out the values and standards that should guide behaviour, although there is no specific mechanism to monitor the implementation of the Code of Conduct. These texts, along with a requirement in primary legislation (ERA 99, schedule 1, point 8) and the Commissioner contracts of employment, foresee that Commissioners are subject to a one year cooling-off period. Similar rules do not exist for staff at the Director level or below, whose contracts are approved by DPER. CRU accounts are audited yearly by the Office of the Comptroller and Auditor General, which reports to the Committee of Public Accounts in the Oireachtas. CRU also presents its accounts to the Oireachtas via the Minister as part of their annual reporting process.

Stakeholder engagement, regulatory quality tools, and appeals

Stakeholder consultation is at the heart of the CRU's decision-making process; it would benefit from a more strategic approach. The CRU implements a consistent, transparent and predictable consultation strategy, and provides feedback to all respondents explaining whether comments have been taken on board. In general, consultation processes are welcomed and positively assessed by the private sector. However, at times the consultation and re-consultation on decisions is felt to be excessive and could be counter-balanced by other good regulatory practices, such as engaging in the early phases of identifying the issue at stake and the various regulatory and non-regulatory options for Regulatory Impact Assessments (RIA). The CRU could also further explore more targeted and innovative approaches to eliciting the views of consumers (and not only the private sector). These approaches could include the use of behaviourally-informed experiments to identify problems faced by consumers and test possible solutions. They could include the use of social media to surveys consumers on a particular issue, as well as the use of consumer fora as sounding boards to elicit the views of consumers (and not necessarily representing them).

The uptake of good regulatory practices by the CRU can support independent decision-making and accountability. The CRU is not legally required to conduct *ex ante* or *ex post* assessments of its regulatory decisions. It has, on a pilot basis, carried out RIA in the case of major policy decisions. Carrying out such assessments and communicating on them transparently would strengthen the CRU's legitimacy and performance management systems, and would ultimately increase trust in the regulator's decisions and knowledge of its activities. Similarly the regulator could undertake *ex post* assessments of its regulatory activities, perhaps on a pilot basis, and communicate on and learn from findings for future work. The appointment of a good regulatory practices Manager to carry forward this agenda within the regulatory agency would be helpful and could help bolster the learning function internally. There may also be value in having a "devil's advocate" approach where Commissioners are faced with difficult or more controversial decisions.

For the majority of CRU decisions, the only appeal mechanism available is through Judicial Review in the Courts. An alternative appeal mechanism for appeals relating to licensing decisions has been available for some time, although the first appeal has only recently been triggered. CRU decisions can generally be appealed by regulated entities only in the Irish Courts and typically in the commercial section of the high court, with a focus on the decision-making process rather than the technical merit of the decision itself. Industry may shy away from using this "last resort" confrontational mechanism that may, in any case, only be accessible to the bigger players as per the cost of the procedure. An alternative mechanism has been available for some time but the first appeal has only recently been lodged. This mechanism allows licensees to appeal modifications to licences, or refusal to award a licence, via an independent appeals panel established specifically for this purpose.

Internal organisation management

The CRU is structured into the Commission (formed by the three Commissioners) and four Divisions that combine technical and cross-cutting operational functions. The CRU Senior Management Team (SMT) is composed of the three Commissioners and four directors of Divisions. The allocation of responsibilities to each division is the results of both organic developments over time and the CRU's intention to maximize efficiency and collaboration across intersection work areas. The Divisions are: Energy Markets, Energy Networks, Energy Safety and Water, with horizontal functions absorbed across Divisions, with Customer Affairs, Communications and Operations functions resting with the Water Division, and Legal resting with Energy Networks, each with a dedicated manager leading the area of work. This structure is not viewed as hindering operations under the current management, as staff appear to communicate fluidly and efficiently across Divisions. Going forward, given the evolution of workloads, eventual changes in management of the CRU and the need for specialised professional leadership for all areas of technical and corporate functions, this structure may need to be revised.

The CRU has recently introduced internal planning and management tools to improve project management outcomes, that could be better linked to strategic planning. In response to a lack of timely implementation of certain projects, the CRU has recently adapted a process for planning and monitoring the implementation of the work programme (Integrated Business Plan, IBP) that allows for automatic generation of update reports for review by the Commissioners as Divisions input the status of their projects into a central IT portal. The Plan is reviewed on a quarterly basis and links the CRU budget and resources to the monitoring exercise.

Recommendations

- *Advocate for more transparent criteria and selection process for CRU Commissioners to be published.* This could include advertising positions and select nominees through an independent search committee submitting proposals to Ministries, possibly with the involvement of the Oireachtas at some stage in the process. This would contribute to a clearer independence framework for the regulator if done systematically.

- ***Instate structured mechanisms for the presentation of CRU annual reports to Oireachtas standing committees.*** Structured and regular engagement with the Oireachtas could be structured around key milestones occurring over the lifecycle of the regulator's planning and reporting activities. These meetings would also provide an opportunity to discuss trends and long-term challenges for the sectors overseen by the CRU in a manner that would be mutually beneficial for the CRU and the Oireachtas. These meetings would not replace topic-specific briefings, ad hoc discussions or other communications to the Oireachtas, but would strengthen the accountability mechanism and the relationship with Oireachtas and provide Members of Parliament with information and insights on issues of particular relevance for Ireland, benefitting the legislative process. As per a more targeted communications strategy, information would be presented to the Oireachtas committees in readable and accessible format. Reports and any supporting information should be shared with the Committees in advance of the hearings to allow for sufficient time to analyse information and prepare eventual questions. The regulator should aim to create a similar "no surprises" relationship that it enjoys with the Department with the legislature.

- ***Strengthen reporting of the SEMC on its activities and outputs in regulating the all island single electricity market.*** Given the uncertain context of Brexit, regular reporting to the respective accountability authorities (for example, the JOC in Ireland) on the decisions of the SEMC and the operation of the all-island market could be beneficial to continued shared governance of the market to demonstrate the benefits of the SEM to the all-island consumer.

Box 3. The role of the parliament in the nomination and/or appointment of Commissioners in France, Italy and Mexico

France's Commission for Energy Regulation (CRE)

The French energy code provides that Board of Commissioners of the Commission for Energy Regulation (*Commission pour la regulation de l'énergie*, CRE) comprises six members, while respecting parity between men and women. The President of the Board is appointed by a decree of the President of the Republic upon proposal of the Prime Minister, following public hearings and a formal opinion on the nominee expressed by the relevant parliamentary committees. Three members of the Board are also appointed by a decree of the President of the Republic, one of them upon proposal of the Minister in charge of the French Overseas Territories based on the person's knowledge and experience of non-interconnected areas. The Presidents of the National Assembly and the Senate appoints two additional members of the Board each (one based on the person's knowledge and qualifications in the field of data protection and the other in the field of local energy services).

Italy's Regulatory Authority for Electricity, Gas and Water (AEEGSI)

The Italian Regulatory Authority for Electricity Gas and Water was established by Law No. 481 of 14th November 1995, which defines the Authority's governance system, including Board structure, appointment mechanism, and members' requisites. Following Law 239/2004, the Authority's Board is composed of five commissioners: the President and four members.

All commissioners are appointed by decree of the President of the Republic following nomination by the Council of Ministers on the basis of a proposal by the Minister of Economic Development. Nominations are submitted to the relevant parliamentary committees for scrutiny, and the appointment is based on a two-thirds majority vote. In 2011, following a spending review which involved all public sector, the number of Board members was reduced from five to three.

The Prime Minister nominates a Chairman, in agreement with the Minister for Communications. The nominee is subject to the binding opinion of the relevant parliamentary committees of the Senate and the Chamber of Deputies, which can hold hearings of the nominee. Following a favourable opinion by two-thirds of the members of each relevant parliamentary committee, the Chairman is appointed by a decree of the President of the Italian Republic. In 2011, following a spending review, the number of Board members was reduced from 9 to 5.

Mexico's Commission for Energy Regulation (CRE) and National Hydrocarbons Commission (CNH)

The CRE and CNH governing councils are appointed by the Senate upon proposals made by the Executive. The hiring process for CRE and CNH President Commissioner and Commissioners is conducted through a short-list of three candidates proposed by the President of the Republic to the Senate, which chooses one of them following hearings and a vote. The shortlist is based in requirements stipulated in the Law of the Co-ordinated Energy Regulators (2014) and it is established by the Executive through informal internal consultations.

Sources: OECD (2016), *Being an Independent Regulator*; OECD (2017a), Driving Performance of Mexico's Energy Regulators; information provided by Italy's Regulatory Authority for Electricity, Gas and Water (AEEGSI) (December 2017).

- *Lead on the uptake of good regulatory practices (impact assessment, ex post evaluation, stakeholder engagement) in a proportional and targeted manner, and use these practices to foment internal learning as well as the advancement of the better regulation agenda within the Irish government.* Filters and quality control checks, for example on the quality of impact assessments conducted for proposed regulatory decisions and or processes for engaging with stakeholder, could ensure that good regulatory practices are integrated into the work of the CRU. The appointment of a good regulatory practices Manager, responsible for quality control and learning and/or a clear responsibility for quality control within one of the existing units/directorates could strengthen the CRU's practices in this area.

- *Continue to actively engage with consumers through dedicated forums, in addition to available channels for online stakeholder consultation.* This active dialogue will be key in areas such as the continued implementation of the water reform, as well as the roll-out of other key programmes in other sectors.

- *Give careful consideration to the possibility of developing an administrative review process of decision-making by the regulator.* The system for the review of the legality and procedural fairness of regulations, and of decisions made by bodies empowered to issue regulatory sanctions, needs to ensure that citizens and businesses have access to reviews at reasonable cost and receive decisions in a timely manner. The experience of the recently triggered appeals panel for licensing modifications and the 2013 Forfas review may provide valuable insight into how alternative appeal mechanisms could function, as well as learnings from the prior communications appeal panels.

- *Map current and future corporate functions and needs (linked to legal, human resource, finance, communication) and identify best organisational structure and resources to support them, in line with work force planning exercises.* The current internal organisation model of the CRU operates well, but this may change according to evolutions in workload, leadership and personnel. The internal organisation model should take into account the need for dedicated specialised leadership in all technical and corporate areas of work of the regulator. Any identified gaps should be addressed to DPER via the parent Departments, built on a Business Case for the regulator's impact and results.

Output and outcome

A large amount of data is requested and collected by the CRU, which is used to inform the work of the regulator but not always to share information about sector performance in a transparent and public manner. The CRU holds the power to request and collect a large amount of information from regulated entities. In the energy sector, entities that account for over 5% of the retail market report a full set of data, those with 1-5% market share report a limited data set, and those under 1% are not required to submit any data. Industry submits data to the CRU through an online system and generally does not feel that requirements are burdensome. A broad range of data is also requested from the electricity and gas network companies in the context of price controls. In the water sector, since 2016 a Framework of reporting performance Metrics has been defined for Irish Water. Irish Water will begin submitting information which will be reviewed and published by the CRU for the first time in 2017, allowing for the creation of a sound baseline for performance in due course. It will be essential for the CRU to have similar data collection rights in the different sectors under its responsibility for it to effectively carry out its mandate.

CRU activities are guided by multiyear year Strategic Plans that focus on policy outcomes, but it is not clear how these Plans are monitored or guide decision-making. The CRU's current Strategic Plan refers to the 2014-18 period and proposes six Strategic goals for this period. Five of the six goals focus appropriately on the policy outcomes of the CRU's mandate, serving as a compass for the CRU's activities during this period, with one out of six goals referring to management of resources and the quality of regulatory processes. The plan attaches measures of success and implementation strategies for each goal, as well as a provision for a regular revision of the goals in rapidly evolving sectoral contexts, but it is not clear how monitoring or reviews are carried out or how they may influence decision-making. The Strategic Plan will cover three years (2019-21) for the next planning period.

The Strategic Plan is operationalised through annual work programmes with comprehensive indicators, but the strategic and operational plans are not fully aligned and the focus of the indicators could be improved. The annual IBP are elaborated internally, based on a mixture of top-down and bottom-up approach. These yearly plans follow a different structure from the Strategic Plan, with five areas that correspond to CRU internal structure rather than the six goals of the Strategic Plan. They include 34 key performance indicators (KPIs) to monitor implementation that were developed in part to respond to a requirement in the 2013 Government policy statement on economic regulation. The KPIs are quite comprehensive as they address performance of the sectors regulated by the CRU and the operations of the CRU, including indicators for mostly outputs and processes. However, the focus of some of the indicators could be improved as they sometimes mix several outputs or outcomes to measure rather than concentrating on one. Moreover, there is some misalignment of the five overall areas of the IBP from the six strategic goals of the Strategic Plan, and of the KPIs of the integrated business plan from the measures of success of the strategic plan. This may result in a duplication of efforts in monitoring or unclear reporting.

Recommendations

- *Ensure the collection of appropriate data from regulated entities to inform CRU reporting and analytical activities.* The CRU holds the power to collect a large amount of data and information from regulated entities in the sectors that it oversees. The CRU should seek to enhance compliance with data submission obligations while ensuring that requests on the regulated entities and processes for submission are as streamlined as possible.

- *Use the Strategic Plan as a tool for reporting on CRU performance and results, and seize the opportunity to use the 2019-21 Strategic Plan to develop such a comprehensive and streamlined performance assessment and reporting framework.* This would involve developing a baseline and reviewing the current set of indicators to link them more explicitly and directly to the high-level measures of success included in the Plan It would allow for all reporting to follow the framework set by the Strategic Plan and would strengthen the narrative and coherence of the CRU's reporting on results, also avoiding duplication of planning and monitoring efforts. The CRU could undertake this exercise in 2018 for the elaboration of its next Strategic Plan that will cover the 2019-21 period.

- *To have a more effective performance matrix for management and steering, align the annual operational plan and its performance indicators to the goals and indicators of the Strategic Plan and ensure that performance indicators collect and provide information that can be used by management to track progress and identify issues for attention for management.* This would enable streamlined strategic planning at all levels of the regulatory agency and avoid duplication of monitoring efforts. It is recommended that the CRU moves away from using KPIs which may be too granular or number-focused, and develop an appropriate set of performance indicators that more effectively measure the effectiveness and impact of the CRU's work, both internally and for presentation to the Oireachtas and also fulfil the requirements of the 2013 Government policy statement on economic regulation.

Box 4. AEEGSI's Performance Indicators & Assessment Framework

The Italian Regulatory Authority for Electricity, Gas and Water (AEEGSI) tracks both service quality (outcomes) and the efficiency and effectiveness of the regulatory process (inputs and outputs). The aim is to improve the regulator's performance and the quality of the services provided to consumers.

Outcomes

The AEEGSI defines outcome indicators to design incentive based regulation and monitor the evolution of the regulated sectors. For instance, AEEGSI has been able to progressively increase the quality of supply through incentives and penalties paid to and by distributors by measuring the average duration of interruptions of electricity supply (yearly minutes of lost supply per consumer).

The AEEGSI conducts an annual review to monitor the evolution of the energy retail markets and eventually adjust regulatory provisions to foster competition and enhance consumer protection. The annual review uses, for instance, the HHI index (Herfindahl-Hirschman Index) to measure competition; the ratio between complaints and served customers to capture the quality of the interaction with energy suppliers; the share of consumers changing their supplier (i.e. switching rate) to track the sector's maturity (consumers' awareness and trust, suppliers' proactivity and the regulatory environment). By assigning a standard cost for unit of energy not supplied, it is also possible to evaluate the direct impact on the final users through a cost-benefit analysis on the consumer side, considering incentives paid to distributors and avoided interruptions.

Inputs and outputs

The AEEGSI links the Strategic and Operational planning process to its objectives, which are assessed in terms of inputs and outputs.

For each objective, inputs are mainly determined by the costs of the employed workforce. On an annual basis, each Department defines the working hours and the relative annual costs an objective has required to be met.

During the regulatory process each deliverable may be considered an output to be associated to an objective. In order to distinguish contributions from different units, production processes have been broken down and intermediate outputs are also considered, as long as they could be identified as final products of specific phases of a process or sub-processes.

Considering the peculiarity of the regulation and the rapidly evolving regulated sectors, a quantitative estimation of output has been centred on the complexity inherent to their realisation. This feature is analysed summing indicators to be assigned in a dedicated IT information system, related to four parameters:

- ***Problem solving:*** it is measured with reference to the necessary professional skills, the discretion applied to solving the case, as well as the ordinary or innovative feature of the case in question.

- ***Effort***: the intensity of the commitment sustained to bring the output to fruition, such as the quantitative dimension of the activities to be carried out, the severity of the approached internal procedure, and the intensity of the interactions with other stakeholders.
- ***Co-ordination among units:*** the need to make use of contribution of other organisational units and from which it is possible to infer a customer-supplier relationship.
- ***Time compression:*** the need to achieve output in a shorter time due to exogenous and unforeseen or foreseeable causes, such as the need to modify the current planning of activities.

Performance assessment is carried out analysing, for each objective, the evolution of input and output indicators through the regulatory period considered in the Strategic and Operational Plans and their correlations to evaluate the overall efficiency and identify potential improvements.

Source: Information provided by Italy's Regulatory Authority for Electricity, Gas and Water (AEEGSI), December 2017.

- ***Simplify and review performance indicators used to monitor performance and delivery of work programmes to focus on measurable deliverables*** on the basis of a more balanced set of IPOO indicators (input, process, output and outcome) (Figure 1). Currently, the CRU has KPIs that are multi-layered/focused, making it difficult to monitor their achievement. IPOO indicators would also need to include indicators that measure the quality of the processes currently used by the CRU and, for example, refocus some of the process indicators that are currently used towards tracking for instance measurement of accuracy, timeliness, accessibility, engagement with stakeholders, risk analysis, use of evidence.

- ***Use data submitted by the industry and generated by the CRU to regularly communicate on sector performance.*** The preparation and communication of regular sector performance reports can be used as an opportunity to engage with industry. Such reports would strengthen the transparency of CRU activities and results and the regulator's results framework.

- ***Develop a simple dashboard of high-level performance indicators that can be used to regularly update the Oireachtas Committees on regulator and sector performance.*** This dashboard can use the one that is being developed for the Integrated Business Plan and be adapted to the information that Members of Parliament would be more interested in, including on key sector trends and results for consumers. Such a tool can strengthen the "no surprises" relationship with the legislature that the CRU will aim to develop and can simplify the Committees' work in reviewing CRU performance.

- ***Pursue the idea of an Output Monitoring group for the water sector which was initiated with other sector regulators but not carried out.*** This would help continue to build synergies between the different regulators of the sector and bring clarity to what is being delivered by Irish Water and when in terms of outputs and outcomes for customers.

Figure 1. Input-process output-outcome framework
for performance indicators

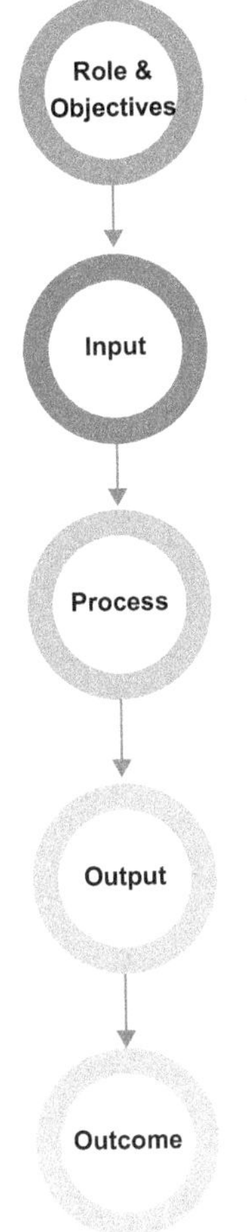

Clearly identified role & objectives
Clear role and set of objectives aligned with functions and powers to inform actionable performance indicators.

Efficiency and effectiveness of Input
Organisational and financial performance (e.g. planned activities completed on time and on budget).

Quality of processes for regulatory activity
Existence and effective use of regulatory tools and processes (e.g. measurement of accuracy, timeliness, accessibility, participation, risk analysis, use of evidence).

Output from regulatory activity
Effective regulatory decision, actions and interventions (e.g. decisions taken which were upheld).

Direct outcome/impact of outputs (e.g. compliance with regulator's decisions).

Wider outcomes — to note that these indicators are meant to be a "watchtower" to loop back and help identify problem areas, orient decisions and identify priorities; they should be used as learning (rather than accountability) indicators:

Market structure
(e.g. level of concentration);

Service and infrastructure quality
(e.g. frequency and reliability of services to consumers, reliability and deployment of infrastructure);

Consumer welfare
(e.g. ability of consumer to choose the service that best fits their preferences);

Industry performance
(e.g. revenues, profitability, investment).

Note: This framework was proposed in the initial methodology for the performance assessment framework for economic regulators (PAFER) discussed with the OECD Network of Economic Regulators (NER). It has been refined to reflect feedback from NER members and the experience of other regulators in assessing their own performance.
Source: OECD (2015), *Driving Performance at Colombia's Communications Regulator*, Figure 3.3 (updated in 2017), OECD Publishing, Paris, http://dx.doi.org/10.1787/9789264232945-en.

Notes

1.   Previously known as the Commission for Energy Regulation (CER).

2.   Electricity sector: Electricity Regulation Act, 1999, and later the Energy (Miscellaneous Provisions) Act 2006 and Electricity Regulation (Amendment) (Single Electricity market) Act 2007; Gas sector: Gas Interim Regulation Act, 2002; Energy safety: (Gas (Interim) (Regulation) Act, 2002; Electricity Regulation Act, 1999 (as amended); Petroleum (Exploration and Extraction) Safety Act 2010 and Petroleum (Exploration and Extraction) Safety Act 2015; Water: Water Services Act 2013, Water Services (No. 2) Act 2013, the Water Services Act 2014 and the Water Services Act 2017.

Chapter 1. Regulatory and sector context

This chapter describes the main features of the sectors regulated by Ireland's Commission for Regulation of Utilities. It also provides an overview of Ireland's public institutions and institutional and regulatory reform.

In December 2015, the Department of Communications, Climate Action and Environment (DCCAE) published a new White Paper on Energy Policy in Ireland, following from the Green Paper on Energy Policy published the previous year. The 2015 policy framework takes into account domestic developments that have taken place since the 2007 White Paper, along with EU and international developments, to set out the actions and measures needed to achieve Ireland's EU 2020 objectives.

The main objectives of the Irish Energy Policy are: security of energy supply, competitiveness, environmental sustainability, and regional integration on the island of Ireland as well as with neighbouring European countries.

The energy sector was one of the targets of the broader national reform that had taken place after the financial crisis. More specifically, Ireland was requested to undergo "an independent assessment of the electricity and gas sectors, taking due account of the European Union regulatory context for these sectors", which was conducted by the International Energy Agency (IEA) in late 2011. The IEA subsequently recommended that Ireland ensures that its energy sector restructuring is compliant with the EU Third Energy Package Legislation (IEA, 2012).

Ireland's ongoing policy development and implementation is also taking into account the package of measures and targets proposed by the European Union's Clean Energy Transition as of November 2016. The EU's "Clean Energy for All Europeans" legislative proposals cover areas including: energy efficiency, renewable energy, electricity market design, security of electricity supply, energy connectivity, clean energy technology, as well as governance rules for the Energy Union. The Commission has also set EU-wide targets such as cutting emissions by at least 40% by 2030 and various other measures to help accelerate the EU's clean energy innovation and transition.

Box 1.1. European energy market integration

The European energy market integration is an ongoing project that aims to foster competition and achieve secure, affordable and sustainable energy supply for EU citizens. It follows the EU Third Energy Package of 2009, which aimed to make the EU's internal energy market fully effective, as well as create a single EU electricity and gas market. The EU Third Package included two Directives and three Regulations that were adopted in July 2009:

- Directive on common rules for the internal market in electricity (2009/72/EC)
- Directive on common rules for the internal market in gas (2009/73/EC)
- Regulation on conditions of access to natural gas transmission networks (2009/715/EC)
- Regulation on conditions for access into the network for cross-border electricity exchange (2009/714/EC)

Regulation on the establishment of the Agency for the Cooperation of Energy Regulators (ACER) (2009/713/EC) EU Member states were mandated to transpose the Directives into national law by 3 March 2011. The Directives and Regulations covered a number of areas relating to electricity and gas trade and governance including: the separation of energy and supply from transmission and distribution networks (i.e. unbundling), wholesale and retail markets, market regulation, network codes, cross-border gas and electricity trade, and consumer protection.

A progress report in 2014 found that the EU energy market integration had helped to reduce wholesale electricity prices by one-third, stabilise gas prices between 2008 and 2012, increase the choice of energy suppliers, encourage construction of energy infrastructure linkages, and increase cross-border trade for both electricity and gas.

In July 2015, the EU introduced a new Energy Union strategy – or commonly called the "Summer Package" – which proposed a redesign of the European power market, an update to energy efficiency labelling, and a revision to the EU emissions trading scheme. The Energy Union strategy aimed to support EU 2030 climate and energy targets, and to enhance the role of renewables in the EU energy market. In November 2016, the EU followed with another package of measures called the Clean Energy Package – or "Winter Package" – which further elaborated proposals to increase the cost-competitiveness, efficiency, security and sustainability of energy supply, as well as improve the co-ordination and governance of the EU energy market (see Box 1.2). Both of these packages are intended to support the completion of the integrated European energy market. As of June 2017, the European Commission is running a public consultation to invite feedback on the EU strategy for cross-border energy networks.

Sources: European Commission (2017), "Markets and consumers: integrated energy markets for European households and businesses"; European Commission (2014), "Single market progress report"; European Commission (2009), "Questions and answers on the third legislative package for an internal EU gas and electricity market".

Box 1.2. EU Clean Energy Package

In November 2016, the European Commission introduced a new package of measures and accompanying documents to help the European Union (EU) advance on a clean and competitive energy transition. The "Clean Energy for All Europeans" proposal – or commonly called the "Winter Package" – focuses on three key objectives: putting energy efficiency first, leading the world in renewable energy, and ensuring a fair deal for consumers. The package covers: electricity market design and integration, security of energy supply, governance of the Energy Union, innovation, energy efficient buildings, eco-design, energy pricing, investment, industrial competitiveness, and transport.

The EU Winter Package is the result of a Commission-led consultation process that began in July 2015, and contains eight new and revised legislative proposals:

- Recast of the Internal Electricity Market Directive
- Recast of the Internal Electricity Market Regulation
- Recast of the ACER Regulation
- Regulation on Risk-Preparedness in the Electricity Sector and Repeal of the Security of Supply Directive
- Recast of the Renewable Energy Directive
- Revised Energy Efficiency Directive
- Revised Energy Performance of Buildings Directive
- Regulation on the Governance of the Energy Union

In February 2017, Ireland's Department of Communications, Climate Action and Environment (DCCAE) launched a public consultation on the EU Winter Package, requesting feedback by 8 May 2017. Presently, Ireland has already set a number of energy targets in alignment with EU targets for 2020, including for renewables, energy efficiency, and climate change (i.e. 20% energy efficiency, 20% renewables penetration;[1] 20% reduction in greenhouse gas emissions).

In particular, a key provision in the proposed regulation on the Governance of the Energy Union requires each Member State to draft a National Energy and Climate Plan for 2021-2030 by 1 January 2018 and finalize this plan by 1 January 2019. This National plan is intended to consolidate existing national planning and reporting from more than 50 existing sectoral plans complying with various EU legislation covering energy, climate and other Energy Union policy areas into one comprehensive and integrated plan and report. The Sustainable Energy Authority of Ireland (Ireland) is supporting the DCCAE in reviewing and providing inputs as appropriate with its statutory remit.

The EU Winter Package feeds into a broader EU programme of over 40 planned measures to strengthen, standardise, and integrate the European Union's energy market. The Winter Package follows the Climate and Energy Package announced in July 2015, and the Energy Security Package in February 2016. Once the European Parliament and the Council agree on a common text and adopt the legislative proposals put forth by the Winter Package, they will become binding EU legislation. Discussions on the new proposals are ongoing as of June 2017.

1. 20% renewables target is binding according to the EU Renewable Energy Directive 2009/28/EC. The 20% targets for energy efficiency and GHG emissions reductions in the EU Energy and Climate Package are non-binding and as agreed at the European Council in December 2008.
Sources: European Commission (2016), "Commission proposes new rules for consumer centred clean energy transition"; Department of Communications, Climate Action and Environment (2017), "Public Consultation on the Clean Energy for All Europeans Package"; Sustainable Energy Authority of Ireland (2017a), "Energy Targets FAQ"; Sustainable Energy Authority of Ireland (2017b), "Joint Oireachtas Committee for Communications, Climate Action and the Environment Opening Statement", February.

Institutions

Ireland is a parliamentary republic headed by an elected President and an appointed Taoiseach (Prime Minister) who heads the Executive Branch, or the Government. The Government consists of no less than seven and no more than fifteen members (ministers) under Article 28 of the Constitution.

Legislative power is held by the Oireachtas, the bicameral national parliament, which comprises the President and two elected houses: the Dáil Éireann (lower house or House of Representatives), the Seanad Éireann (upper house or Senate).

All Acts of the Oireachtas begin life as Bills, which are proposals for legislation. Bills that are applicable to the general body of citizens are called Public Bills and those that are promoted by local authorities and private bodies or individuals for their own purposes are called Private Bills. Private Bills are very rare and have their own procedures. Before a Government Bill is initiated in the Dáil or Seanad, its contents will have been approved by the Government. A process of consultation with Government Departments and groups likely to be affected by the Bill will have taken place beforehand. Sometimes, the Government will publish a Green Paper, which will be a discussion document in which it sets out its idea and invites feedback from individuals and relevant organisations. Legislation will generally be initiated in either House by the Government, although parliamentary procedures also allow Opposition parties and Independent Members to introduce Bills that are called "Private Members' Bills". For the most part, Private Members' Bills do not succeed in progressing beyond the Second Stage debate, although a few have in fact become law. The President cannot veto Bills passed by the Oireachtas but may refer them to the Supreme Court of Ireland, should questions arise about the Bills' compliance to the Constitution.

A separate process exists for the development of statutory instruments. Legislation gives powers to certain bodies (such as the CRU) to propose secondary legislation, and sets out a process whereby this type of legislation becomes law. Essentially, secondary legislation may come into force by laying the proposed legislation before the House of the Oireachtas for 21 days, after which the statutory instrument comes into law.

The Supreme Court is the court of final appeal in Ireland and is headed by the Chief Justice. Judges are appointed by the President after being nominated by the Government.

Institutional and regulatory reform

Following the financial crisis of 2008, a New Economic and Recovery Authority (NewERA) was established under the National Treasury Management Agency in September 2011, with the responsibility to provide centralised financial and commercial advisory services and act as a dedicated source of corporate finance advice to Ministers of the Government. NewERA was also tasked with assessing and reforming the state's management and shareholding arrangements in companies in which the state holds majority stake. In the energy sector, such companies included ESB, Bord Gais (now Ervia), EirGrid, Bord na Mona, and Coillte. NewERA was assigned to carry out corporate governance functions for these companies, including reviewing capital investment plans and potential synergies between them. After the Irish government agreed to the asset divestment programme as part of the EU-ECB-IMF programme, NewERA was tasked with advising on the disposal of state assets and, if appropriate, overseeing any restructuring of state companies in co-ordination with the Minister for Public Expenditure and Reform.

Box 1.3. Financial crisis and reform post-2008

Ireland was severely impacted by the financial crisis in 2008, after more than a decade of property-led boom. Ireland entered into an EU-ECB-IMF financial assistance programme in 2008 and, in 2010, received a EUR 85 billion financial support package from EU member states through the European Financial Stability Fund (EFSF) on the condition that it would undertake fiscal policy and structural reforms, including on the energy and water sectors. Ireland implemented a National Recovery Plan in 2011-14, successfully delivering a large number of complex reforms quickly. The Irish government also strengthened its institutional framework with a new independent fiscal council, fiscal rules, reformed public employee service and activation policies, a vocational training authority, a stronger competition authority, a new agency to facilitate knowledge transfer, and increased transparency and openness in government.

Ireland exited the EU-ECB-IMF financial assistance programme in December 2013. Overall, Ireland's economy has been rebounding strongly after the crisis, recording a GDP growth of 5.2% in 2014, the fastest in the OECD, buoyed by strong export gains and employment growth. This high level of growth continued through 2016, and the unemployment rate dropped significantly to below 7% in early 2017. Wage growth coupled with contained inflation has increased the level of household disposable real income, and going forward, solid domestic demand is expected to contribute to broader economic growth in Ireland alongside export demand.

In 2017 and 2018, the economy is projected to grow at a more moderate pace. Despite improved employment prospects for educated participants in the labour force, long term unemployment remains high, with women over 30 and lower educated segments of the population underrepresented in the labour market. As the labour market tightens, strong wage pressures are expected to fuel higher inflation. While the sustained performance of multinational companies based in Ireland have helped drive the initial stages of post-crisis recovery in the country, small and medium-sized enterprises have lower levels of competitiveness, productivity and R&D spending. Overall, businesses are expected to expand at a slower pace than in previous years, given already high labour costs and high levels of external uncertainty, in part attributable to the ongoing discussions about Brexit.

Source: OECD (2015), *OECD Economic Surveys: Ireland 2015*, OECD Publishing, Paris; OECD (2017), "Ireland Economic Forecast Summary", June, OECD, Paris.

In the water sector, as part of the Programme of Financial Support for Ireland (with the EU, the IMF, and the ECB), the Government committed to carrying out an independent assessment of a transfer of responsibility for public water and wastewater services from local authorities to a national water services authority, with a view to commence charging domestic customers for those services. The Government published an implementation plan to reform the public water sector in 2012. Subsequently, a national water service provider – Irish Water – was established as a subsidiary of Ervia under the Water Services Act (amended 2013) and as a company under the Companies Act. CRU became the designated the economic regulator of Irish Water and, at the time, aimed for the utility to become self-financing over time via envisaged water charges for domestic customers.

In 2004, the Department for Enterprise, Trade and Employment launched a Government White Paper on Better Regulation, "Regulating Better", which outlined six key principles of better regulation (necessity, effectiveness, proportionality, transparency, accountability and consistency) and an agenda of 50 actions under 5 headings:

- The legislative process and statue law revision
- RIA and evidence-based policy making
- Institutional change and review
- Sectoral regulators/sectoral issues
- Regulatory procedures and processes

A progress report published by the Taoiseach in 2007 identified several key challenges faced by Irish regulatory agencies: Regulatory impact assessment; Simplification and accessibility of the law; Administrative simplification; Public consultation; A framework for the effective functioning of regulatory agencies; Stronger framework for the management of EU regulations; and Enforcement and compliance.

In December 2008, the National Competitiveness Council published a Smart Economy Strategy (Building Ireland's Smart Economy – a Framework for Economic Recovery) which included "Smart Regulation" as one of five key action areas. In particular, this report emphasised the need to reduce the cost of doing business and remove barriers to competition in locally traded sectors of the economy.

Box 1.4. Government Policy Statement on Sectoral Economic Regulation

The Government Policy Statement on Sectoral Economic Regulation was published in July 2013, endorsed by then Prime Minister Enda Kenny of the Fine Gael party. The Statement follows a review by Forfás[1] to identify ways to enhance the efficiency and cost-competitiveness of sectoral regulators, and the effectiveness of economic regulation in general, The Statement aimed to design a strategic regulatory framework to guide national policy objectives, as well as help sectoral Departments prioritise and balance national and sectoral objectives. The Statement additionally calls on sectoral Ministers to introduce legislative changes that would provide for:

- Setting a hierarchy of objectives that prioritises national objectives
- Requiring policy/mandate reviews of economic regulators at least every seven years, on a statutory basis
- Establishing a performance and accountability framework for regulators and regulated sectors

According to the Statement, Ministers and Departments would lead the implementation of the strategic framework pertaining to their sector. Sectoral Ministers were requested to set out detailed implementation of the framework by October 2013, with the outputs monitored and reviewed continuously thereon by the Department's annual output statements, annual reports, and the annual Action Plan on Jobs.

1. Forfás was the national policy advisory board for enterprise, trade, science, technology and innovation until August 2014, when its functions were merged into the Department of Jobs, Enterprise and Innovation (DJEI). The DJEI subsequently became responsible for the annual Action Plan on Jobs.
Source: Taoiseach (2013), Regulating for a Better Future: A Government Policy Statement on Sectoral Economic Regulation, July.

Ireland has also taken important steps to enhance the governance and performance of its regulators, including instating a statutory review of economic regulators every seven years, following the Government Policy Statement on Sectoral Economic Regulation published by the Taoiseach in 2013.

Ireland implements a comprehensive Code of Practice for the Governance of State Bodies to enhance governance, accountability and transparency. The Code of Practice was issued in 1992 by the Department of Finance and updated by the Department of Public Expenditure and Reform (DPER) in August 2016. The updated Code of Practice also applies to independent regulatory bodies, with the details of its application to arms-length entities currently being defined. The implementation of the Code of Practice to the CRU is under the auspices of the DCCAE's newly created centralised corporate governance Division.

Box 1.5. Code of Practice for the Governance of State Bodies in Ireland

In August 2016, the Department of Public Expenditure and Reform published an updated set of guidelines on the Code of Practice for the Governance of State Bodies (hereafter "the Code"). The Code serves as a framework for the application of best practices in corporate governance by commercial and non-commercial State bodies. State bodies, all trading subsidiaries and joint ventures of State bodies are required to confirm compliance with the Code or otherwise justify adjusted applications or exemptions to the relevant line Minister or parent Department(s). All regulators in Ireland are therefore required to comply with this Code.

The original Code was established in 1992, and updated in 2001, 2009 before the latest version in 2016. The current Code covers the following topics:

- Roles, Effectiveness and Codes of Conduct for the Board, Chairperson and Board Members
- Business and financial reporting requirements
- Guidance for Audit and Risk Committees
- Relations with the Oireachtas, Minister and parent Departments
- Remuneration, Superannuation, and Official Entitlements
- Customer Service Quality

Source: Department of Public Expenditure and Reform (2016), Code of Practice for the Governance of State Bodies, August.

An OECD assessment of Ireland in the Better Regulations in Europe report showed that the Better Regulations agenda was still active in 2010, albeit incomplete. The agenda had encountered challenges rallying support from different parts of the administration. Communication and awareness-raising on the importance of Better Regulations was lacking and the agenda needed additional support to be mainstreamed into policymaking in Ireland, particularly after the 2008 financial crisis when a number of weaknesses in the regulatory and supervisory frameworks of Ireland were revealed. The review also recommended scaling up the use of ICT tools and further developing e-Government as a supporting element of Better Regulation (OECD, 2010).

The OECD Regulatory Policy Outlook for Ireland (2015c) found that RIA is conducted for all primary laws and all major subordinate regulations. By contrast, stakeholder engagement is only formally required in the development of some primary laws and subordinate regulations; there are no requirements to open consultations to the general public. *Ex post* evaluations are conducted only for some primary laws; there are no automatic evaluation requirements. In the Outlook, Ireland scores below the OECD average for engagement and *ex post* evaluations (OECD, 2015c).

References

CER (2014), "Strategic Plan 2014-18: Regulating Water, Energy and Energy Safety in the Public Interest", Commission for Energy Regulation, Dublin.

Department for Enterprise, Trade and Employment (2004), "White Paper on Regulating Better", https://dbei.gov.ie/en/what-we-do/business-sectoral-initiatives/reducing-administrative-burdens/better-regulation/.

Department of Communications, Climate Action and Environment (2017), "Public Consultation on the Clean Energy for All Europeans Package", www.dccae.gov.ie/en-ie/energy/consultations/Pages/Consultation-on-Clean-Energy-Package.aspx.

Department of Communications, Climate Action and Environment (2015), "White Paper on Energy Policy in Ireland", https://www.dccae.gov.ie/documents/energy%20white%20paper%20-%20dec%202015.pdf.

Department of Communications, Climate Action and Environment (2014), "Green Paper on Energy Policy in Ireland", https://www.dccae.gov.ie/documents/dcenrgreenpaperonenergypolicyinireland.pdf.

Department of Communications, Climate Action and Environment (2007), "White Paper on Energy Policy in Ireland", https://www.dccae.gov.ie/documents/1_EnergyWhitePaper12March2007.pdf.

Department of Public Expenditure and Reform (2016), "Code of Practice for the Governance of State Bodies", August, www.per.gov.ie/en/revised-code-of-practice-for-the-governance-of-state-bodies/.

Department of Taoiseach (2004), "White Paper Regulating Better".

Department of Taoiseach (2013), "Regulating for a Better Future: A Government Policy Statement on Sectoral Economic Regulation", www.taoiseach.gov.ie/eng/publications/publications_2013/policy_statement_on_economic_regulation_2013.pdf.

EirGrid (2017a), "All Island Interconnection Imports and Exports", July, http://smartgriddashboard.eirgrid.com/#all/interconnection.

EirGrid (2017b), "Celtic Interconnector", July, www.eirgridgroup.com/the-grid/projects/celtic-interconnector/the-project/.

European Commission (2017), "Markets and consumers: integrated energy markets for European households and businesses", https://ec.europa.eu/energy/en/topics/markets-and-consumers.

European Commission (2016), "Commission proposes new rules for consumer centred clean energy transition", https://ec.europa.eu/energy/en/news/commission-proposes-new-rules-consumer-centred-clean-energy-transition.

European Commission (2014), "Single market progress report", https://ec.europa.eu/energy/en/topics/markets-and-consumers/single-market-progress-report.

European Commission (2009), "Questions and answers on the third legislative package for an internal EU gas and electricity market", http://europa.eu/rapid/press-release_memo-11-125_en.htm?locale=en.

IEA (2016), "Ireland Balances for 2014", www.iea.org/statistics/statisticssearch/report/?country=ireland.

IEA (2012), "Energy Policies of IEA Countries – Ireland 2012 Review", https://www.iea.org/publications/freepublications/publication/energy-policies-of-iea-countries---ireland-2012-review.html.

Mutual Energy (2017), "Capacity of the Moyle Interconnector, Mutual Energy", www.mutual-energy.com/electricity-business/moyle-interconnector/trading-across-the-moyle-interconnector/.

OECD (2017), "Ireland Economic Forecast Summary", June, OECD, Paris.

OECD (2017b), *Driving Performance of Mexico's Energy Regulators*, OECD Publishing, Paris http://dx.doi.org/10.1787/9789264267848-en.

OECD (2015), *OECD Economic Surveys: Ireland 2015*, OECD Publishing, Paris, http://dx.doi.org/10.1787/eco_surveys-irl-2015-en.

OECD (2015b), *Driving Performance at Colombia's Communications Regulator*, OECD Publishing, Paris, http://dx.doi.org/10.1787/9789264232945-en.

OECD (2015c), *OECD Regulatory Policy Outlook 2015*, OECD Publishing, Paris, http://dx.doi.org/10.1787/9789264238770-en.

OECD (2015d), OECD Survey on the independence of economic regulators, OECD, Paris.

OECD (2010), *Better Regulation in Europe: Ireland 2010*, OECD Publishing, Paris, http://dx.doi.org/10.1787/9789264095090-en.

SEM Committee (2017a), "Overview", https://www.semcommittee.com/overview.

SEM Committee (2017b), "SEM Monitoring Report Q4 2016", https://www.semcommittee.com/sites/semcommittee.com/files/media-files/mmu%20public%20report%20q4%202016.pdf.

Sustainable Energy Authority of Ireland (2017a), "Energy Targets FAQ", www.seai.ie/energy-data-portal/frequently-asked-questions/energy_targets_faq/.

Sustainable Energy Authority of Ireland (2017b), "Joint Oireachtas Committee for Communications, Climate Action and the Environment Opening Statement", February. www.oireachtas.ie/parliament/media/committees/communicationsclimatechangenaturalresources/presentations/cleanenergypackage/2017-02-28-SEAI-Opening-Statement.pdf.

Chapter 2. Governance of the Commission for Regulation of Utilities

The Performance Assessment Framework for Economic Regulators (PAFER) was developed by the OECD to help regulators assess their own performance. The PAFER structures the drivers of performance along an input-process-output-outcome framework. This chapter applies the framework to the governance of Ireland's Commission for Regulation of Utilities (CRU) and reviews the existing features, the opportunities and challenges faced by the CRU in developing an effective performance assessment framework.

Role and objectives

The CRU is an independent multi-sector regulator with a range of economic, customer and safety functions and duties. It was initially established as the Commission for Electricity Regulation (CER) by the Electricity Regulation Act, 1999; however, as its mandate increased, the Commission updated its name to become the Commission for Regulation of Utilities (CRU) in 2017. Today, its sectoral responsibilities include the following:

- Electricity: Electricity Regulation Act, 1999, and later the Energy (Miscellaneous Provisions) Act 2006 and Electricity Regulation (Amendment) (Single Electricity market) Act 2007;
- Gas: Gas Interim Regulation Act, 2002;
- Energy Safety: (Gas) (Interim) (Regulation) Act, 2002; Energy (Miscellaneous Provisions) Act 2006; Petroleum (Exploration and Extraction) Safety Act 2010 and Petroleum (Exploration and Extraction) Safety Act 2015;
- Water: Water Services Act 2013 and Water Services (No. 2) Act 2013, the Water Services Act 2014 and the Water Services Act 2017.

The CRU's positive track record in introducing competition, regulating pricing and delivering cost-competitive electricity and gas has contributed to decisions to expand its mandate to energy safety and water as well. The addition of new roles and functions, along with frequent amendments to existing legislation (particular in the energy sector and in relation to EU directives) have resulted in a complex and fragmented legislative framework governing the CRU's operations.

The CRU operates in the framework of a Strategic Plan (2014-18) that sets the following key priorities:

- Safe supply of energy and gas
- Ensuring the security of electricity supply from production to consumption
- Ensuring the security of and gas supply, including diversification of resources
- Ensuring the reliability of clean water supply and efficient wastewater treatment
- Fair energy pricing
- Regulations according to international best practice.

In addition, the CRU defines a more detailed work programme annually. The 2017 work plan identifies the following key priority areas of work, each of which has a set of key performance indicators (KPIs):

- Energy safety
- Energy networks
- Water regulation
- Energy markets
- Corporate services and customer support.

Table 2.1. Main features of sectors regulated by the CRU

	Public Water and Wastewater	Energy		
		Petroleum Safety	Electricity	Natural gas
Number of service providers/utilities	Irish Water	Petroleum producers: 2	Transmission and Distribution Operators: 2 Licensed suppliers (Residential and Commercial. Industrial) : 9	Transmission and Distribution Operators: 1 Licensed residential suppliers: 64 Licensed industrial and commercial suppliers: 8
Market Structure	Single national utility responsible for delivery of all public water services including: drinking water treatment and distribution; and collection, treatment and disposal of waste water	N/A	Prices deregulated in retail market Prices deregulated in wholesale market spanning two jurisdictions (Ireland and Northern Ireland) and two states (Ireland and the United Kingdom) [Single Electricity Market]ESB provides 47% of power generation to the all-island market, supplying roughly 1.4 million customers TSOs and DSOs ESBN and EirGrid - are state-owned (natural monopolies)It was mentioned during the fact finding mission that EirGrid is responsible for maintaining the Grid Code (transmission) and ESBN are responsible for maintaining the Distribution Code; both under regulatory oversight of CRU. EirGrid is responsible for the implementation of EU Network Codes covering markets, grids with regulatory oversight by the CRU.	Prices deregulated in retail markets Prices deregulated in wholesale market BGE and ESB are the largest shippers of natural gas
Price setting role of the CRU	The CRU approves the charging policy and associated tariffs for non-domestic customers of Irish Water. The CRU is charged with approving an appropriate funding requirement sufficient to enable the utility to deliver the required services to specified standards in a cost efficient manner. The CRU also approves Irish Water's connection policy for water and wastewater which includes the basis for charges to both domestic and non-domestic customers for connections to Irish Water's network.		CRU approves revenues for the two electricity network companies (ESB as DSO and TAO and EirGrid as TSO) through a price control process carried out every five years. The current price review period is from 2016 to 2020.	CRU approves revenues for the gas network company (Gas Networks Ireland as both the DSO and TSO) through a price control process carried out every five years. The fourth price control (PC4) was decided in September 2017

Source: Information provided by the CRU, 2017.

Table 2.2. Main Irish state-owned energy and water enterprises

	Annual turnover (2015, in EUR)	Number of employees (2015)
Electricity Supply Board (ESB)	4 791 million (2016)	7 000 (7 600 in 2016)
ESB Networks (ESBN)	Falls under ESB	
EirGrid	706.2 million	
Bord na Mona	433 million	Over 2 000
Ervia* (water, gas distribution, dark fibre; previously Bord Gais, renamed 2014)	1.342 million	1 404
Irish Water (subsidiary of Ervia)	851.1 million	495

Note: The Department of Housing, Planning and Local Government (DHPLG) is the shareholder for Ervia Group.
Source: Information provided by the CRU, 2017.

Electricity

The CRU was first established as the Commission for Electricity Regulation (CER) by the ERA 1999, which authorised the regulator to: grant licences to generate and supply electricity as well as authorise the construction of generation stations; permit access to transmission and distribution systems by licence holders or eligible customers; monitor and regulate the wholesale and competitive retail electricity market. In 2007, the ERA was amended to give CRU authority to oversee the rights and obligations relating to electricity trade in the all-island Single Electricity Market (SEM).

The Electricity Regulation Act (1999; as amended) assigned the following functions to the CRU:

- Grant licences to generate and supply electricity
- Authorise the construction of generation stations
- Grant access to transmission and distribution systems by licence holders or eligible customers
- Monitor and regulate the competitive wholesale and retail electricity market
- Oversee the rights and obligations relating to electricity trade in the all-island Single Electricity Market (SEM)
- Advise the Minister on, *inter alia*, development of electricity and gas industries, on retail market monitoring and exercise of ministerial function under the gas and electricity regulatory legislation.

In 2005, the CRU began to phase out the regulation of tariffs in the retail electricity market. Progressive price deregulations for various consumer segments in the retail electricity market were carried out between 2005 and 2011.

The CRU regularly audits the compliance of electricity and gas suppliers according to the Electricity and Natural Gas Suppliers' Handbook (CRU, 2017c). The Handbook comprises individual Codes of Practice that cover key customer protection items including: billing, disconnections, marketing, pre-payment meters, and vulnerable customers. The CRU chooses the specific aspects of the market to audit and either audits all suppliers active in that retail market or, in some cases, a particular supplier that has been flagged by a customer complaint or irregular market or data reporting.

The CRU regulates the revenues that can be recovered by network monopolies EirGrid (Transmission System Operator or TSO), ESB Networks (Transmission Asset Owner or

TAO), and ESB Networks Ltd (Distribution System Operator or DSO) for providing access to transmission and distribution networks for energy suppliers. Energy suppliers may choose to pass on these costs to customers. The CRU sets the allowable revenue to reflect a combination of reasonable cost recovery of the DSO, TSO and TAO, as well as international benchmarks for comparable network operators and owners. The transmission revenue is collected by the TSO and distributed between the TSO and TAO as per SI445 of 2001 and the Infrastructure Agreement between the two bodies. The CRU conducts price reviews every five years while setting allowable revenues and tariffs every year within a price control period.

Ireland has a renewable energy target of 40% by 2020, to which a Public Service Obligation (PSO) levy and an updated renewable energy feed-in-tariff (REFIT) programme will contribute. The CRU is responsible for calculating and certifying the annual PSO levy to support electricity generation from sustainable, renewable and indigenous sources, as mandated by the DCCAE and approved by the European Commission. The calculation of the PSO levy is expected to increase in complexity going forward. When the PSO levy was first introduced, there was only one company holding renewable energy contracts. Now there are 56 companies holding renewable contracts, considerably increasing the CRU's work load in this area, and role clarity of the existing legislation will be needed.

Gas

In 2002, the Commission's remit was expanded to include the regulation of the natural gas sector. Similar to its functions in the electricity sector, the CRU became responsible for granting licences to ship and supply natural gas, permitting access to gas transmission and distribution systems by licence holders or eligible customers; and overseeing the monitoring and regulation of the wholesale and retail gas markets.

The Gas Act (Interim 2002) assigns the following functions to the CRU:

- Grant licences to ship and supply natural gas
- Provide access to gas transmission and distribution systems to licence holders or eligible customers
- Monitor the competitive development of gas supply
- Monitor the development and effectiveness of the competitive gas retail market, including tariffs to customers.

In 2005, the CRU began phasing out the regulation of tariffs in all sectors of the retail gas market. Progressive price deregulations for various consumer segments in the retail gas market were been carried out between 2005 and 2014, when the prices for residential customers were de-regulated.

The CRU is responsible for regulating charges in the natural gas market under the Gas (Interim) (Regulation) Act 2002. The CRU sets the tariffs for transporting gas through the transmission and distribution networks, which are operated by Gas Networks Ireland. The CRU regulates the level of revenue Gas Networks Ireland can recover from customers by setting the level of revenue to reflect reasonable cost recovery and international benchmarks against comparable TSO/DSOs.

Energy safety

The CRU is responsible for the designation and oversight of the safety supervisory bodies charged with monitoring gas installers and electrical contractors with respect to safety under the Energy (Miscellaneous Provisions) Acts 2006 and 2012. Where offences are identified under the Act, the CRU can and does undertake prosecutions.

The CRU is responsible for regulating the activities of natural gas and LPG undertakings with respect to safety under the Energy (Miscellaneous Provisions) Acts 2006 and 2012. This is carried out under the Gas Safety Framework, which covers shipping, supply, storage, transmission, distribution and use of natural gas, as well as with regard to certain specified LPG undertakings. The CRU's main functions include safety licensing, compliance assurance (carrying out audits and inspections), incident investigations and enforcement.

The CRU is also responsible for upstream petroleum safety, including offshore safety under the Petroleum (Exploration and Extraction) Safety Acts, 2010 and 2015. The CRU's main functions here include safety permitting, compliance assurance (carrying out audits and inspections), incident investigations and enforcement.

Water

In 2013, the water sector (residential water and public wastewater services) was added to the CRU's mandate through the passing of two Water Services Acts, which outlined the functions and duties of the regulator as follows:

- Serve as the economic regulator of Irish Water in the provision of water services, although there are no specific regulatory duties assigned to CRU in this Act. The Act more generally ascribes the CRU permission to "do all such things [following Section 27] as may be necessary or expedient for the purposes of the performance by it of water regulatory functions under any enactment passed after the passing of this Act."
- Advise the Minister in relation to the development of policy regarding the regulation of the provision of the water services
- Fixing charges for water services and approving or requiring changes to the water charges plan
- Specify minimum standards of service by Irish Water
- Protect the interests of water consumers
- Approve, reject or modify codes of practice on the standards of performance by Irish Water, including in relation to issues of billing and provision of information to customers
- Direct Irish Water to comply with approved code of practice
- Consult with Irish Water regarding its water services strategic plan
- Request Irish Water to provide information as the CRU reasonable requires to perform its functions
- Determine/approve the duration of Irish Water's capital investment plans
- Comply with Ministerial policy directions
- Enter into a co-operation agreement with the EPA
- Finalise a Water Statement of Strategy.

In 2014, further legislation outlined additional functions/duties of the CRU in the public water sector:

- Provide a dispute resolution mechanism for customers of Irish Water
- Act as Secretariat for the newly established Public Water Forum.

The CRU may approve or reject water charges proposed by Irish Water with or without changes. According to Section 22 of the Water Services (No. 2) Act 2013, Irish Water may prepare and submit to the CRU a 'water charges plan' that specifies the calculation of water charges to customers for the provision of water services, reflecting the costs likely to be incurred by Irish Water in performing these functions. Irish Water may also propose different charges to different customers for the provision of water services, subject to the approval of the agreement by CRU. The Minister may issue policy directions, to which the CRU has a legislative duty to comply under Section 42 of the Water Services (No. 2) Act. One such direction has been issued to date regarding water charges, in July 2014.

Inspection and compliance

The CRU carries out annual Supplier Audits to monitor compliance with the Electricity and Gas Supplier Handbook. The most recently published audit report was the 2016 CRU Audit of Compliance with the Code of Practice on Vulnerable Customers. The CRU expects its inspection and compliance related activities to increase in the near future.

The CRU has the power to conduct unannounced visits to retrieve documents, review and/or collect information from regulated entities in the energy sector. Inspections are typically carried out on entities that have been flagged as a risk or potential risk from company or market data.

The CRU carries out audits and inspections of the designated safety supervisory bodies to ensure compliance with the CRU safety supervisory scheme. At the close of 2015, there had been a total of 4 successful prosecutions since the introduction of Restricted Electrical Works into the Safe Electric regulatory scheme and 26 successful prosecutions since the introduction of the RGI regulatory scheme.

The CRU carries out a safety audit and inspection regime for the gas sector as part of its annual work programme as the regulator in charge of energy safety. The topics selected for review under the Audit and Inspection regime are chosen with consideration to previous audit and inspection findings, incident reports and safety case risk ratings. A total of 11 audits and inspections were carried out by the CRU on Gas Networks Ireland in 2015 (Information provided by the CRU, 2017). Findings from inspections are recorded on an internal database but not made public. In the case of prosecution, the CRU issues a press release. As inspections may lead to prosecutions, these findings are not published. Enforcement actions taken are reported publically in the CRU annual reports.

The CRU carries out an audit and inspection regime for the petroleum sector as part of its annual work programme. The topics selected for review under the Audit and Inspection regime are chosen with consideration to previous audit and inspection findings, incident reports and safety case assessments. 6 audits and inspections were carried out by the CRU on petroleum undertakings in 2016. Findings from inspections are recorded on an internal database, but the reports are not made public. Enforcement actions taken are reported publically in the CRU annual reports.

The Water Services (No. 2) Act provides the CRU with the power to request information as it "may reasonably require" in order to perform its statutory functions, and provides that Irish Water shall comply with such as request "as soon as reasonably practicable". However, the CRU does not have the power, as in electricity or gas, to conduct unannounced visits to retrieve documents, or to review and/or collect information from Irish Water. Furthermore, unlike the companies in the energy sectors, Irish Water does not operate under a licence; therefore, the CRU does not have the legal powers associated with licensing or sanctioning Irish Water as it does in other sectors under its mandate. The CRU has expressed interest to standardise its authority to request information from regulated entities across the energy safety, electricity, gas, and water sectors.

The regulator has recently been granted sanctioning powers to fine certain but not all regulated entities in case of non-compliance, but how these powers will be used is currently being defined. Up to now, the CRU can only address non-compliance through notices or, in the most extreme case, licence revocation. Sanctioning powers are not applicable to Irish Water as of September 2017.

Single electricity market

The SEM Committee (SEMC) regulates the wholesale single electricity market of Ireland and Northern Ireland (Box 2.1). The Committee consists of three Commission for Regulation of Utilities representatives (the three Commissioners), three Utility Regulator representatives, an Independent Member and a Deputy Independent Member (SEMC, 2017). Legally, the SEMC is not cross-jurisdictional but rather two committees that meet at the same time, although in effect the same members of the committees make decisions for the all-island market. Correspondingly, there is no joint oversight mechanism for the SEMC in legislation; rather, an All-Island Joint Steering Group provides an oversight function, and regulators may individually or jointly appear before relevant bodies responsible for oversight in either jurisdiction (Northern Ireland or Ireland).

The All-Island Joint Steering Group (JSG) comprises representatives of the CRU, UR, DCCAE and the Department for the Economy in Northern Ireland (DfE).[1] The main roles of the JSG are to facilitate policy consistency across both jurisdictions, and monitor implementation of SEMC decisions. The official terms of reference for the JSG calls for it to "maintain progress and ensure that developments in both jurisdictions complement the central goal of the mutually beneficial integrated system." Meetings of the JSG take place on a quarterly basis. The future and the governance of the SEMC may be impacted by the form of Brexit, but this is uncertain at this time.

Box 2.1. All-Island Single Electricity Market

The United Kingdom (UK) and Ireland signed a Memorandum of Understanding (MOU) in 2006 to support the establishment of an all-island Single Electricity Market (SEM) that would link the wholesale electricity markets of Ireland and Northern Ireland, as well as legislation in both countries. The SEM and its corresponding governing authority – the SEM Committee (SEMC) – were established in 2007. Until the Moyle Interconnector between Northern Ireland and Ireland was built and operational, the two power markets of Northern Ireland and Ireland operated separately, with the power market of Northern Ireland operating as part of the UK system.

The creation of the SEM was broadly supported across government, industry and consumer groups in Ireland and Northern Ireland, as well as by the UK government. It was viewed to bring about many benefits including: increased security of energy supply, improved efficiency and cost-effectiveness for electricity dispatch, and greater competition in the wholesale electric markets which could help bring down prices.

The SEM functions as a pool market in which all electricity suppliers and generators above a minimum threshold are obliged to trade electricity. Generators bid into the pool market according to their short-run marginal costs, and a System Marginal Price (SMP) is determined for every half-hour according to a stacking of generator cost bids (starting from the least expensive) until the all-island customer demand is met. This facilitates the dispatch of the most competitively priced electricity to customers. All generators that are scheduled to run in the market are then paid the same SMP for the electricity they supply, in addition to a separate Capacity Payment for any periods that they are available to generate, which help contribute to generators' fixed costs. In case of constraints in the pool, generators may be dispatched in a different order than the market schedule, with constrained plants compensated for the costs of out of market operations.

The SEM is considered to be a relatively concentrated market, with Ireland's Electricity Supply Board (ESB) accounting for the largest share of installed capacity (46%) as well as the largest share of the spot market (47.5%) in the SEM.

The SEM is operated by the Single Electricity Market Operator (SEMO), which is run as a joint-venture by two transmission system operators in Ireland (EirGrid) and Northern Ireland (SONI). SEMO is responsible for administering the market, which includes calculating the SMP, paying generators and invoicing suppliers.

The SEM is regulated by the SEMC, which comprises representatives from the Irish Commission for Regulation of Utilities (CRU) and the Northern Ireland Authority for Utility Regulation (UR), as well as an independent member and a deputy independent member, all of whom work together to ensure the effective delivery of policy decisions related to SEM matters. The stated goal of the SEMC is to protect consumer interests on the island of Ireland by effectively promoting competition between persons engaged in, or commercial activities pertaining to electricity trade through the SEM.

In physical terms, the electricity grids of Ireland and Great Britain are currently connected by two High Voltage Direct Current (HVDC) interconnectors: a 500 MW Moyle interconnector connecting Northern Ireland and Scotland (owned by Mutual Energy), and another 500 MW East West interconnector connecting Ireland and North Wales (developed and owned by EirGrid). Capacity on both interconnectors is sold via auction. As of June 2017, the East West interconnector is operating at full 500 MW capacity, while the Moyle interconnector is operating at 250 MW due to long-running cable faults.

The TSOs in Ireland and France are also exploring another HDVC interconnector between the two countries called the Celtic Interconnector, which would have an import-export capacity of 700 MW. If built, this subsea interconnector between the south coast of Ireland and the north-west coast of France will become Ireland's only direct energy link to an EU member state once the United Kingdom exits the European Union. In addition, a proposal for a further 500MW interconnector between Ireland and the United Kingdom, the Greenlink project, is being progressed by a private sector developer.

Presently, the SEM is undergoing an update in order to better integrate with the emerging single wholesale electricity market in Europe, which aims to start operations in May 2018. The SEMC is developing a new market design for the SEM called an Integrated SEM (I-SEM) which will facilitate coupling with the rest of the European power market via interconnectors with Great Britain. I-SEM aims to bring wholesale trading arrangements in line with European power trading models as established in the EU Third Energy Package, which requires several core changes to the SEM design including a significantly different system for Capacity Payments. Phase I and II of the I-SEM concluded in September 2014 with a high level design for the new I-SEM (SEM-14-085a). The I-SEM project is now in Phases III and IV of detailed design and implementation.

It is worth noting that, following the exit of the United Kingdom from the European Union, that the I-SEM market may face uncertainties in its operation and designs going forward. In the meanwhile, progress on the Celtic Interconnector between Ireland and France continues with financial support from the European Commission, which has designated the linkage as a "Project of Common Interest" for a more integrated electricity system in Europe.

Sources: SEM Committee (2017), About Us; SEM Committee (2017b), SEM Monitoring Report Q4 2016; Mutual Energy (2017), Moyle Interconnector; EirGrid (2017a), All Island Interconnection Imports and Exports, July; EirGrid (2017b), Celtic Interconnector, July.

Co-ordination

Co-ordination with other government and regulatory institutions

Table 2.3. Co-ordination in gas and electricity sectors

Authorities	Mandate (in relation to regulation of the sector)	Perimeter of activity	Areas of joint competencies with the CRU
Single Electricity Market (SEM) Committee	Electricity Regulation Amendment (SEM) Act 2007Electricity (Northern Ireland) Order 2003 as amended.	SEM matters in which the SEM Committee has a relevant function. The SEMC is able to decide on what is a SEM matter. Regulation of the all-island wholesale electricity market is undertaken through the SEM Committee which is a cross jurisdictional committee of the CRU and Utility Regulator in Northern Ireland.	SEM matters in which the SEM Committee has a relevant function.
Department of Communications, Climate Action, Environment (DCCAE)		Facilitate the development of communications and energy infrastructure and markets that contribute to sustainable economic and social development	DCCAE develops policy in the energy and climate change space, which is implemented by the CRU.DCCAE is also responsible for transposing EU directives to national law in the electricity and gas sector, which is then implemented by the CRU There is good quality interaction with the Department on the development of energy policy and regulations.
Joint Steering Group of Department of Economy, Northern Ireland and the Department of Communications, Climate Action and Environment	Memorandum of Understanding between the Government of the United Kingdom of Great Britain and Northern Ireland and the Government of Ireland December 2006		Pursuant to MoU the Authorities will consult each other on electricity matters within their respective jurisdictions that materially affect or are likely to materially affect the SEM.
Competition and Consumer Protection Commission (CCPC)	The statutory body responsible for enforcing consumer protection and competition law in Ireland. It is also responsible for enforcing EU competition laws in Ireland.		The CRU must ensure customers are benefitting from competition and are duly protected. Where this is not the case the CRU must take action. The CCPC enforces general completion law and customer protection law and may take action also. Generally, the CCPC looks to the CRU for matters relating to the electricity and natural gas sectors. There is an MoU
Data Protection Commissioner	Data Protection Legislation		

Source: Information provided by the CRU, 2017.

Table 2.4. Co-ordination in energy safety

Authorities	Mandate (in relation to regulation of the sector)	Perimeter of activity	Areas of joint competencies with the CRU
DCCAE	Economic w/ some environmental e.g. EIS	Onshore and offshore Issues all petroleum authorisations first step in process for persons wishing to carry out petroleum activities in Ireland.	Economic V Safety. International best practice has these functions required to be separated. Some crossover in data assessed but assessments made for different reasons. Some joint competencies on infrastructure design. MOU being drafted.
Health and Safety Agency (HSA)	Occupational Health and Safety	Onshore and offshore	Inspects all the same infrastructure for different safety reasons i.e. occupational V major accident hazards. MOU in place
Environment Protection Agency (EPA)	Issuance of enviro permits such as IED/IPPC licences and Dumping at Sea licences for decommissioning	Onshore and limited offshore	Limited. MOU in place, focus on the development of the safety framework and, since 2017 revision, on water functions (see below)
Marine Survey Office (MSO)	MSO regulate maritime transport at sea and on inland waters. Key areas are: Safety; Security; Ship sourced pollution prevention.	MSO and CRU interface where a vessel is within the 500m safety zone, or carrying out a designated petroleum activity (i.e. at the well or the proposed well or production location).	Both bodies assess vessels associated with petroleum activities to varying degrees with regards to safety. MOU in place currently being updated.
Irish Coast Guard (IRCG)	Responsible for response to, and co-ordination of, maritime accidents which require Search & Rescue and Counter Pollution & Salvage operations. It also has responsibility for approving oil spill contingency plans (OSCP) where offshore drilling is proposed.	Offshore petroleum activities e.g. drilling and production from fixed platforms	IRCG approve the OSCP. This approval is required by CRU to accept related safety cases. Both parties involved in incidents IRCG as first responders and CRU as incident investigators. MOU in place currently being updated.
Irish Aviation Authority (IAA)	IAA regulates safety standards within the Irish civil aviation industry. Relevant functions are the Issuance of Certificates of Airworthiness and Licensing of Aerodromes (helidecks)	All aircraft associated with petroleum infrastructure and activities. Licensing of some petroleum infrastructure helidecks	Overlap in the assessment of petroleum infrastructure in the form of helidecks. CRU does not regulate aircraft in transport, only 500m zone around petroleum infrastructure. Incidents within this area could be investigated by both parties. MoU in place

Source: Information provided by the CRU, 2017.

Table 2.5. Co-ordination in public water and waste water services

Authorities	Mandate (in relation to regulation of the sector)	Perimeter of activity	Areas of joint competencies with the CRU
Environmental Protection Agency (EPA), Statutory Body	Environmental regulation and drinking water and waste water quality regulation.	Enforcement of legislation (both EU and national); licensing; consumer guidance related to water services; dispute resolution	Monitoring Irish Water's delivery of services, including delivery of capital investments and associated outcomes and outputs given respective roles and responsibilities as economic regulator and as environmental regulator. EPA has dispute resolution function for unresolved complaints re water quality, wastewater, and pollution incidents; the CRU has dispute resolution function for complaints covered under customer charter, handbook, and codes of practice. MoU in place between the CRU and EPA which addresses co-operation and information sharing between the bodies.
Department of Housing, Planning and Local Government (DHPLG), Ministry	Develops and implements relevant Government policy and legislation. Oversees the governance of Irish Water, the funding of the utility and delivery of capital investments and services to customers. Lead department regarding the development and implementation of the River Basin Management Plans under the WFD and reporting to the EU regarding these matters.	The Minister is one of three shareholders in Irish Water and has a statutory role in oversight/approval of: • Water Services Strategic Plan (WSSP) Minister approves/refuses to approve Business Plan • Capital grants/investment (Minister may approve grants, giving consideration to most recent investment plan) • Borrowing and guarantees of borrowing and reporting (Minister has joint responsibility to approve with DCCAE and DPER) • Form of accounts (Minister can approve with consent from Minister for DCCAE and DPER) • Account reporting and auditing (Minister may request audit with consent of Minister for DCCAE and DPER) The Minister may issue a policy direction to Irish Water. The Minister's shares do not carry voting rights.	Minister approves Irish Water's objectives, priorities and targets under the WSSP. The CRU reviews Irish water's proposed capital investment plan and associated governance process and targets as part of the review Irish Water's proposed revenue requirement on a periodic basis. The Minister may issue a policy direction to the CRU and the CRU must comply. The CRU sets the allowed revenue for Irish Water on a periodic basis. This is co-funded by Government and through charges to customers where these are in place. The Department monitors Irish Water's performance and delivery under the WSSP and the five-year Business Plan. The CRU monitors IW performance for allowed revenues including associated targets pertaining to capital and operational expenditure. The CRU may request regulatory accounts from Irish Water as economic regulator. The Department requests accounts from Irish Water in required form given its role.
Department of Public Expenditure and Reform (DPER)	Financial oversight of Irish Water	The Minister has a statutory role in oversight/approval of: • Borrowing (Minister has joint responsibility to approve with DCCAE and DHPLG) • Form of accounts (Minister for DHPLG to approve with consent from Minister for DCCAE and DPER)	The CRU does not share competencies with DPER. DPER engages with DCCAE and DHPLG to set the overall staff numbers in the CRU, with terms and conditions for staff approved by DPER in line with public service norms. The CRU had engaged in significant consultations concerning the water portfolio with the NewERA, which is under this department.

Authorities	Mandate (in relation to regulation of the sector)	Perimeter of activity	Areas of joint competencies with the CRU
		Account reporting and auditing (Minister for DHPLG to approve with consent from Minister for DCCAE and DPER)	
Department of Communications, Climate Action, and Environment (DCCAE)	Financial oversight of Irish Water Develops and implements policy regarding energy including energy efficiency of public sector bodies. Develops and implements policy regarding climate change.	The Minister has a statutory role in oversight/approval of: • Borrowing (Minister has joint responsibility to approve with DPER and DHPLG) • Form of accounts (Minister for DHPLG to approve with consent from Minister for DCCAE and DPER) • Account reporting and auditing (Minister for DHPLG to approve with consent from Minister for DCCAE and DPER)	The CRU does not share competencies with the DCCAE, but acts with regard to the obligations on Irish Water to meet requirements pertaining to energy efficiency and any obligations in relation to climate change. The DCCAE engages with DPER to set the overall staff numbers in the CRU, with terms and conditions for staff approved by DPER in line with public service norms.
Department of Finance, Ministry	Financial oversight of Irish Water	The Minister is one of three shareholders in Irish Water and has a sole or joint statutory role in oversight/approval of: • Borrowing • Provision of monies from the Central Fund • Form of accounts • Reporting and auditing of accounts The Ministers shares do not carry voting rights.	The CRU does not share competencies with the Department of Finance.
Competition and Consumer Protection Commission	Enforces consumer protection laws and regulations	The Consumer Protection Acts in Ireland set out regulations against unfair commercial practices, price displays and controls, customer codes of practice.	Both the CRU and the CCPC enforce consumer protection; the CRU through the Irish Water customer handbook and codes of practice, and the CCPC through Irish consumer protection law.

Source: Information provided by the CRU, 2017.

Co-ordination with other governments and the European Union

The United Kingdom and Ireland signed a Memorandum of Understanding (MOU) in 2006 to support the establishment of the Single Electricity Market (SEM). Prior to the operationalisation of the Moyle Interconnector between Ireland and Northern Ireland, Northern Ireland operated its electricity market as part of the UK while Ireland operated its own market separately. Following legislation in both countries in 2007 establishing the SEM, the CRU assigns representatives to the SEM Committee (SEMC) together with the Northern Ireland Authority for Utility Regulation (UR), with which it jointly oversees the regulatory framework for the wholesale electricity market in the SEM.

Previously, the CRU and the UR had been leading a project called the Common Arrangements for Gas, which seeks to operate the gas systems on a single all-island network basis. However, the project has since been overtaken by the European Network Codes, which require implementation of enhanced trading arrangements across all Member States. Ireland would need to continue co-operation with the United Kingdom and European Commission to ensure that regulatory decisions beyond Ireland's border do not negatively impact its gas market.

Box 2.2. National Smart Metering Programme

In late 2007, the CRU launched the first of a five-phase National Smart Metering Programme (NSMP) to assess the costs and benefits of introducing smart meters to provide dynamic records of electricity and gas consumption to energy providers, as well as receive instructions to switch electricity supply on or off. In 2009-10, Electric Ireland (ESB) and the Sustainable Energy Authority of Ireland (SEAI) conducted a trial that installed smart meters in over 5 000 residential homes and small and medium sized enterprises (SMEs). Results of this trial showed that customers responded positively to smart meters by reducing electricity consumption and their costs, and a decision was taken in July 2012 to roll out energy meters for all residential homes and SMEs in Ireland.

In January 2013, Phase II of the NSMP advanced high level design and procurement of smart meters, and the CRU subsequently published a Decision which outlined the high level function, methodology, objectives and pricing structure. Phase III followed in 2015 with a focus on procurement planning and building activities for suppliers. Phase IV on building and testing was originally scheduled for late 2018, with full deployment of smart meters by 2020. However, following technical delays on procurement and a review of the programme, the CRU and ESB announced in October 2017 that the rollout would proceed on a phased basis, with the first 250 000 meters to be delivered in 2019 and 2020.

Source: CRU (2017), Overview of Smart Meters and information provided by CRU, December.

As part of Ireland's efforts to achieve its decarbonisation goal and align with the EU Clean Energy Package, the CRU has introduced a Strategic Innovation Fund as part of the electricity networks price control (PR4) which seeks to facilitate and incentivise the transformation of the DSO to ensure inter alia:

- Flexible DSO operation including TSO-DSO Interaction
- Electrification of transport
- Flexibility in power systems
- Resilient smart electricity grid used to defer capex investment
- Demand-side response which plays a role in managing imbedded generation, leveraging smart meters (Smart Grids)

Relations with the executive

Participation in the legislative process

CRU makes official submissions on key national and EU policies relating to energy, and engages in informal discussions with the Ministry/DCCAE. The CRU also participates at ACER meetings and provides input to relevant issues in the European context through that platform.

The CRU has the power to make regulations concerning the electricity sector under the Electricity Regulation Act 1999 (amended). The CRU drafts statutory instruments where legally allowed.

Regarding EU-level energy legislation, the DCCAE primarily relies on CRU to provide technical input and guidance.

The CRU can advise the Minister on, *inter alia*, development of electricity and gas industries, on retail market monitoring and exercise of ministerial function under the gas and electricity regulatory legislation.

Executive summary

The Commission for Regulation of Utilities (CRU) is an independent multi-sector regulator with a range of economic, customer and safety functions and duties in Ireland's energy and water sectors. The CRU is a high-performing and well-regarded regulator that has, since its creation in 1999, successfully absorbed new functions and developed and implemented major policy reforms for the benefit of Irish consumers and the country's economy.

As the regulator continues to implement complex projects in a rapidly changing and uncertain policy context, its institutional and organisational capacity to operate effectively needs to be bolstered through integrated reforms to upgrade some of its external and internal governance functions, including strategic planning and human resource management mechanisms.

Role and objectives

The CRU is an independent regulator under the aegis of two Ministries (Department of Communications, Climate Action and Environment, DCCAE and Department of Housing, Planning and Local Government, DHPLG) and is governed by a series of sector-specific laws that have been amended over the years. Currently, the CRU is responsible for regulating energy markets, energy safety, and public water and wastewater services in Ireland. The CRU also shares cross-jurisdictional responsibilities for regulating the all-island Single Electricity Market (SEM), covering Ireland and Northern Ireland.

The CRU has built cordial and predictable ("no surprises") working relationships with the executive and other government entities. However, the gradual increase in the CRU's functions and the complex legal framework in which it operates make it difficult for both stakeholders and the regulator itself to fully understand the CRU's priorities. Moreover, while the regulator's activities are guided by five year Strategic Plans that focus on policy outcomes, it is not clear how these Plans are monitored or how they guide decision-making.

Key recommendations

- Assert the leadership of the CRU in setting its priorities as a multi-sector economic and safety regulator, using the next Strategic Plan (2019-2021) as an opportunity to do so; explore the possibility of setting up an advisory group that can act as sounding board for the definition of the Plan and annual work programmes.

- Strongly advocate for and contribute to the launch of a rationalisation of the CRU's legislative framework in the energy sector.

Minister shall cause to be laid before each House of the Oireachtas a statement of the reasons for such removal." To date no Commissioner has been removed from office.

In the energy sector, the DCCAE formulates policy and legislation for the electricity and gas markets, which serve as a guideline for the activities and targets of the CRU. The CRU also provides informal feedback to DCCAE on legislation and takes part in formal consultation processes. The CRU and DCCAE operate on a "no surprises" basis that entails frequent and regular informal and formal interactions on energy and regulatory issues.

In the energy sector, national regulation is largely governed by European regulation; this is not the case for water, although adherence to the Water Framework Directive is referred to in CRU Water legislation, section (39)(2) of the Water Services Act (No.2), 2013. The cross-jurisdictional remit of the CRU in the case of the Integrated Electricity Market is seen to enhance the independence of the regulator in its decisions for the energy sector.

In the water sector, the DHPLG sets policy and legislation, is a shareholder in Irish Water and oversees the governance and funding of the national utility. The CRU, as economic regulator of the utility, approves its allowed revenue, associated charges where they are in place, and codes of practice regarding its customer service. CRU also works with the Environmental Protection Agency (which is under the aegis of the DHPLG), with whom the CRU has a Memorandum of Understanding and discusses water issues in structured meetings every quarter.

In the water sector, as in the energy and electricity sectors, legislation foresees that the CRU can advise the Minister in relation to the development of policy in the regulation of the sector. During the water sector reform process, the CRU made numerous written submissions to a Special Joint Committee on the Future Funding of Domestic Water Services, and was called to appear six times to provide presentations and answer questions from the Oireachtas. The CRU has a legislative duty to comply with Ministerial policy directions. To date, one such policy direction has been issued regarding water charges in July 2014.

In all sectors that the CRU regulates, it formally provides a work plan including financial information to the Oireachtas, the Irish Parliament, via the DCCAE who lays it before the Oireachtas. This reflects the requirements of the legislation for communicating such documents to the Oireachtas. Likewise, its annual reports are laid before the houses of the Oireachtas but there is no formal approval process by either the Ministry or the Oireachtas. The CRU is entirely funded by revenue from the regulated sector and its annual budget is presented for information to the executive and legislative.

The CRU generally enjoys a good public image and is perceived as independent from the executive, although as implementing government policy the CRU sometimes becomes the public face of policy that it has minimal part in developing. This perception can be exacerbated by the in-depth stakeholder consultations that the Commission also organises, in addition or complementary to the consultations led by the DHPLG e.g. on water reform and river basin management.

Relations with the regulated sector

The CRU implements inclusive and transparent consultation processes via its website in which the regulated industries can take part. All consultations are published, along with explanations from the CRU on which decisions were taken and why.

The CRU may engage in early stage consultation with key stakeholders before the online consultation, depending on the topic.

For consumer representatives, the CRU has established the Customer Stakeholder Group, the Public Water Forum (as required by legislation), and the Non-Domestic Water User Group as formal consumer consultative groups. The CRU also engages with consumers through public consultations.

As Irish Water is the only public industry operator in Ireland, the CRU continuously engages with Irish Water directly on both a formal and informal basis.

Input

Financial resources

The CRU is funded entirely through levy and licence fees from relevant electricity, gas, petroleum safety, and water industry participants. Levies from market participants comprise the bulk of the CRU's income. The relevant undertakings that are liable to paying levies are described as follows:

- Electricity levy from any person engaged in the functions of electricity generation, transmission, distribution and supply;
- Gas levy from any person engaged in the functions of natural gas transmission, distribution or supply. An LPG levy was added in 2015;
- Petroleum safety levy from any relevant petroleum safety activities since May 2013;
- Water levy on Irish Water, in turn funded by government revenue and/or charges where in place.

A number of changes to funding regulations for the CRU have been made in the recent three years, in correspondence with the expansion of the CRU's statutory functions and the need to ensure effective allocation of resources per function.

Table 2.6. Summary of changes to funding regulations 2015-17

Sector	Funding Category	2015	2016	2017
Electricity	Levy: Transmission, Distribution, Supply, Generation	✓	✓	✓
Electricity	Licence Fees (> 1% per annum)	✓	✓	✓
Gas	Levy: Transmission, Distribution, Shippers	✓	✓	✓
Petroleum Safety	Levy: Establishment Costs (SEPIL & Kinsale)	Ends	n/a	n/a
Petroleum Safety	Levy: Operational Costs	✓	✓	✓
Petroleum Safety	Levy: Well Work Safety Case	✓	✓	✓
LPG Safety	Levy: Operational & Licence Fees	✓	✓	✓
Water	Levy: Irish Water	n/a	✓	✓

Source: Information provided by the CRU, 2017.

In general, across senior management it is felt that the CRU disposes of sufficient financial resources to meet its strategic objectives and targets. Constraints are more to do with how these funds can be used on human resources.

The CRU sets its own budget without requiring government participation, in line with the Schedule to the Electricity Regulation Act 1999 (amended). There is no direct government contribution to the CRU budget and the regulator's annual budget is approved by the Commission without approval or *ex ante* assessment by the Oireachtas. In this sense, the CRU has the highest financial independence by statute of any economic regulator in Ireland.

Annual budgets for the electricity, gas, petroleum and water are allocated by the CRU to each sector. Revenues, expenses and capital expenditure directly incurred by each sector are recorded in the separate budgets of the electricity, gas, petroleum and water sectors. Shared costs are allocated to each sector in proportion to the staff numbers engaged in the relevant sector. Costs linked to shared administrative functions such as finance, HR, IT, and Communications are pooled for all sectors. A common budget for contingency is also shared between the sectors underpinned by a risk assessment, to enhance the CRU's financial flexibility beyond the once-a-year opportunity to set the budget, and serve as a buffer to any unexpected work including litigation. Where annual expenditures exceed revenue, the balance is offset against the levy income for the subsequent year. Table 2.7 provides a summary of the annual operating budgets and expenditures of the CRU in the recent three years.

Table 2.7. Annual operating budgets and expenditures at CRU 2015-17 (million EUR)

Year	Electricity	Gas/LPG	Petroleum Safety	Water	Total
INCOME					
2015 (Actual)	8.6	4.7	4.8	2.7	20.8
2016 (Actual)	6.7	3.8	3.1	2.6	16.2
2017 (Budget)	9.7	2.8	1.0	1.9	15.4
EXPENDITURE					
2015 (Actual)	6.9	4.0	2.0	2.0	14.9
2016 (Actual)	8.7	4.1	2.1	2.0	16.9
2017 (Budget)	11.0	3.9	1.7	2.9	19.5

Source: Information provided by the CRU, 2017.

The balances for the electricity, gas, petroleum and water sectors are recorded in their respective accounts, and audited on an annual basis by the Office of the Comptroller and Auditor General, which reports to the Public Accounts Committee of the Oireachtas. The CRU also conducts an annual internal audit, which is outsourced to an audit company).

In general, the CRU's procurement process is obligated to comply with EU Procurement Directives as transposed into law by the Department of Public Expenditure and Reform. The Office of Government Procurement commenced operations in 2014 and, has responsibility for sourcing all goods and services on behalf of the Public Service. In general, for amounts under EUR 5 000 EUR the CRU can directly procure goods and services; for amounts between EUR 5 000 EUR and EUR 25 000 EUR the CRU can use a restricted procurement procedure; for amounts above EUR 25 000 the CRU has to carry out an open tender on the central government website with the process taking up to two months; and for amounts above the EU threshold of EUR 209 000 EUR the CRU has to carry out an open tender for a longer period with the whole process taking 4-6 months. The CRU can use an accelerated procurement process for urgent requirements e.g. services that may be required for safety cases.

The Senior Financial Manager of the CRU is responsible for: core internal financial services including budgeting and accounting; procurement support services (2006 to date); integrated business planning and risk (since 2015); project management and support (2016); the administration of the pension scheme as well as trusteeships.

Human resources

The CRU's overall staff headcount is approved by the Department of Public Expenditure and Reform (DPER), according to the government's Employee Control Framework (ECF), introduced as part of the public sector reforms following the financial crisis. These sanctions are issued to CRU parent departments by DPER at the beginning of each year. Changes are advocated via a Business Case that is presented by the parent Department(s) to DPER, as part of the overall envelope under the jurisdiction under the parent Department (i.e. the parent Department may be obliged to make trade-offs between different entities that it oversees). Typically, the CRU would advocate for additional headcount with its parent Departments and by extension DPER when it takes on a new function, and generally has not sought to increase headcount outside of these occasions. The CRU supplements internal staff expertise with support of specialist consultants where required, for example, to deliver major projects such as I-SEM, the National Smart Metering Project, and the establishment of the Water Regulatory Framework.

**Table 2.8. Sanctions on staff headcount by DPER
for 1 January to 31 December 2017**

DCCAE headcount	90
DHPLG headcount (water only)	15
Total headcount	105

Source: Information provided by the CRU, 2017.

The CRU workforce has steadily increased from 78 full time employees in 2013 to 103 as of May 2017 in line with the increasing functions given to CRU. Professional staff account for more than 80% of total staff.

Table 2.9. Breakdown of CRU supporting and professional staff

Year	Number of supporting staff	Number of professional staff	Total workforce
2017	24	77	101[1]
2016	22	80	102
2015	23	76	99
2014	20	73	93
2013	17	60	77

1. Total headcount for 2017 as of May 2017 does not add up to 105 as some posts are not filled.
Source: Information provided by the CRU, 2017.

Nearly 80% of professional staff is comprised of technical staff (Table 2.10).

Table 2.10. CRU professional workforce

Job family/description	Number of total professional staff (not including supporting staff)
Communication	1
Economics	43
Inspection	6
Legal	3
Managerial	21
Statistician	1
Other (human resources)	4

Source: Information provided by the CRU, 2017.

The CRU has achieved a high level of female representation across the organisation. Female staff count outnumbers male staff count at every professional level, even in the absence of specific HR policy to this aim.

Table 2.11. Breakdown of male and female employees according to staff categories (2016)

Staff category	Male	Female
Senior Management	3	4
Technical Staff	36	40
Support Staff	1	17
Total	40	61

Note: Total headcount for 2017 as of May 2017 does not add up to 105 as some posts are not filled.
Source: Information provided by the CRU, 2017.

Historically, staff retention and terms and conditions for hiring flexibility appear to be the principal human resource challenges, rather than the cap on staff count, although this may change in the future as the scope of work of the CRU expands. The CRU follows government remuneration policy (scaled down following the 2008 crisis) and, as such, the CRU's pay scales are generally not competitive with those offered by industry especially at less senior grades. The terms and conditions of hire, as well as salary scales, are defined by DPER in line with public sector norms which are considered to lack flexibility to compete with industry. All positions have to be appointed at the bottom of the salary scale, which challenges efforts to recruit more experienced staff. Overall, the CRU faces challenges to recruit staff with industry experience that are above entry level, and CRU employees are more likely to take up positions in industry than the inverse. Despite holding open recruitment campaigns to attract senior external candidates with sectoral experience in recent years, vacancies have primarily been filled by internal candidates – the latter of which has not necessarily been a negative as CRU reports that staff have felt encouraged by internal promotion opportunities. Hiring technical expertise in safety has also been a challenge due to salary scales.

To address this challenge, in January 2016, the CRU restructured its salary scale following approval from DPER to include two levels for the position of analyst (analyst and senior analyst), allowing for the hire of analysts at a higher starting salary (Table 2.12). Salaries of all staff recruited since January 2016 comply with the new salary scale.

Table 2.12. CRU salary scales (EUR) before and after January 2016

Grades	Pre-January 2016	Post-January 2016
Senior Manager	73 987-96 047	83 000-98 000
Manager	63 401-88 423	65 000-88 000
Senior Analyst	N/A	47 458-60 224
Analyst	29 922-61 422	33 247-48 593
Graduate Scale	29 922-32 026	30 221-32 020
Admin B Scale	27 831-49 373	27 831-47 975
Admin C Scale	22 638-36 591	22 638-36 591

Source: Information provided by the CRU, 2017.

The shortfalls in staff capacity or inability to easily hire staff on flexible terms to meet temporary demands have led to the CRU relying on external consultants in certain areas. The CRU reports drawing especially heavily on consultants for major projects outside of the annual planning cycle, such as the five-year pricing review, judicial reviews, or unexpected safety cases that suddenly draw away existing staff resources. The heavy reliance on consultants can at times pose difficulties in terms of knowledge transfer, continuity of institutional memory.

Staff turnover rate at the CRU has been perceived to be high, averaging around 11% between 2010 and 2015, and reaching 15% during that period. Turnover is especially severe at the junior levels, as newly trained CRU staff become increasingly attractive to industry which can offer much higher salaries. Since 2016, the staff turnover rate has decreased to 6%, which the CRU attributes to a number of factors including the renewal of the leadership team, the restructuring of pay scales, and greater efforts to improve workplace flexibility and promote staff training and development. However, contracts pre-January 2016 could include a performance-related payment of up to 15% (averaging 7.5% across the organisation), which could no longer be applied to new contracts. It is anticipated by the CRU that where there is no flexibility on terms and conditions and where the CRU staff are attractive to industry, retention of staff will continue to be a challenge, particularly as the economy picks up.

The CRU senior management team meets to discuss human resource management across the organisation and work force planning as needed. The HR team also issues recruitment plans for each year. To assess and plan for current and future staff capacity and performance, the HR team aims to complete competency frameworks for all grades in the CRU and develop an integrated skills matrix for the 2018 planning cycle. The CRU recently launched a new three-year HR strategy in June 2017.

All of the CRU's permanent staff below director level (inclusive) is recruited through open competition by the CRU. Interviews panels can vary dependent on the positions. Psychometric tests or written tests have been given during the recruitment process, although they are not routinely used. Screening and interviews are typically conducted with two Directors and one HR staff, depending on the grade.

Within its allowed annual budget, the CRU offers a number of training and development opportunities for its staff including: in-house courses, knowledge transfer sessions, external courses relating to specific areas of work, including managerial skills, and general health and safety training courses. The CRU also runs a graduate programme for new graduates. Each year, a number of analysts complete the Annual Training on

Regulation of Energy Utilities at the Florence School of Regulation and a water regulation training course for staff operated by the Hungarian regulator.

Staff performance objectives are set in January of each year, with an interim review in June and a final review of performance for the year in December. The CRU follows best practice with respect to performance assessment. There is no formal 360 degree performance review process, although this is offered periodically to members of the Senior Management Team and may be considered for other grades in the future.

Half of the CRU staff are currently employed under contracts that include performance-related pay, which was part of the original pay model when the CRU was established. This component of pay is being phased out following engagement with DPER since January 2016.

Process

Decision making

The CRU has a three-person Commission responsible for setting the strategic direction for the CRU, monitoring its performance, and ensuring CRU's compliance with the law as well as the organisation's constitution and policies. The Commission also represents the CRU with respect to national and EU institutions. The CRU does not have a non-executive Board.

Commissioners are appointed by the Minister, sometimes but not always following a competitive procedure. In the case of the latter, this is run by the Irish Public Appointments Commission on behalf of DCCAE. Commissioners' terms are prescribed in legislation (Electricity Regulation Act, 1999) as being no less than five and not more than seven years, usually five. Their mandates can be renewed once, for a total maximum number of years of ten. Commissioners' terms are staggered so that no more than one vacancy should arise in any one twelve month period. The Chair of the Commission is selected by the Minister from the serving Commissioners on a rotating basis for a period of typically two to three years, but there is no prescribed term for this.

Each Commissioner is assigned lead areas and responsibilities for the benefit of an effective division of tasks (Figure 2.1).

The Commissioners make all key policy decisions, which are taken collectively and, in the case of a vote, by simple majority. Commission decisions are often based on proposals and recommendations prepared by CRU Directors and staff. Clear and predictable functioning of the Commission is set out in in the Commission Rules and Procedures, approved on 1 May 2013 (CRU, 2017b). This foresees inter alia that two members of the Commission form a quorum. In the current composition of the Commission, decisions are made on a consensual basis and have not been put to a vote. Each Commissioner has lead responsibility for specific technical and managerial areas; these rotate between the Commissioners ensuring a high level of engagement in the quality of decisions. Commissioners may delegate authority to Directors as appropriate for technical decision making.

Figure 2.1. Lead areas assigned to CRU Commissioners, as at October 2017

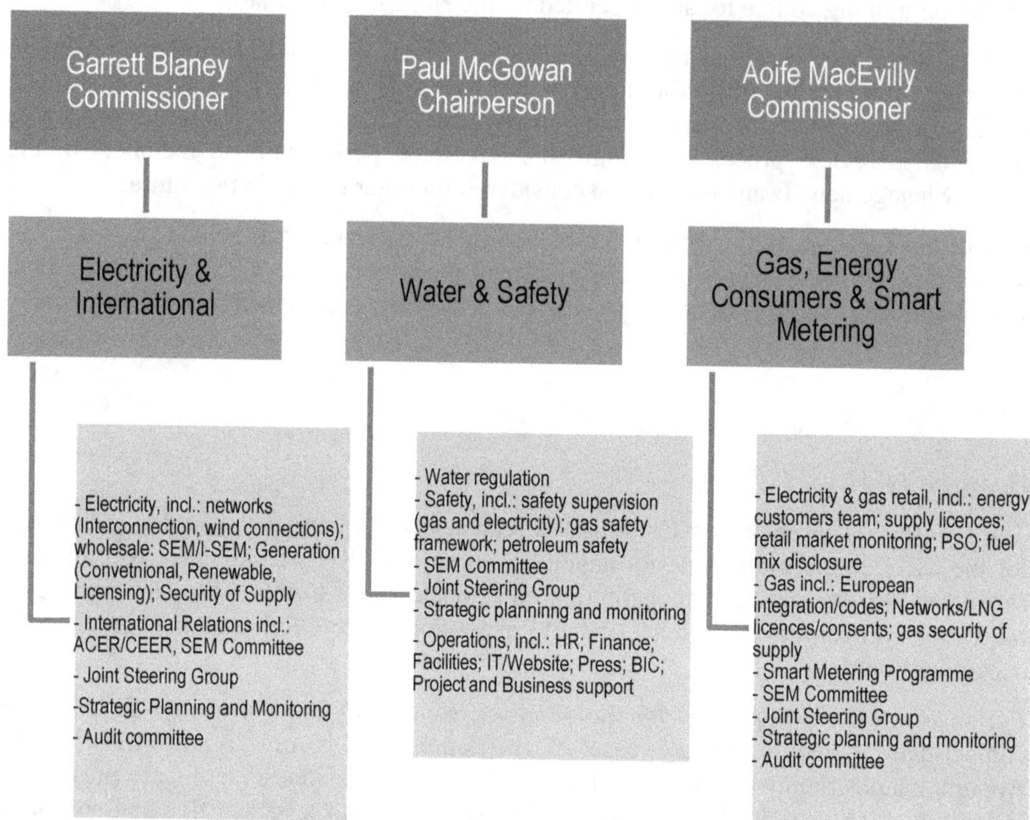

Source: Information provided by the CRU, 2017.

Apart from key policy decisions, Commissioners may also delegate decision-making authority to Directors as appropriate, based on custom and practice. For example, the Commissioners handled the first few safety cases at the CRU, whereas now safety cases are more often handled by Directors.

The Commission meets once a week in meetings chaired by the Chairperson, together with Directors. Presently, three Commissioners and four Directors comprise the Senior Management Team (SMT). Where appropriate, Managers may also join the weekly Commission meeting.

Organisational structure

The CRU is led by three Commissioners (one of whom is appointed as Chairperson of the Commission), in place of a Board. Below the Commissioners are four Directors, each of whom leads a division. The divisions are structured according to the substantive areas of work of the Commission (Water, Energy Markets, Energy Networks, and Energy Safety) with horizontal Corporate Service functions absorbed across the Divisions (Customer Affairs and Operations with Water, and Legal with Energy Networks) (Figure 2.2).

Figure 2.2. Internal structure of the CRU

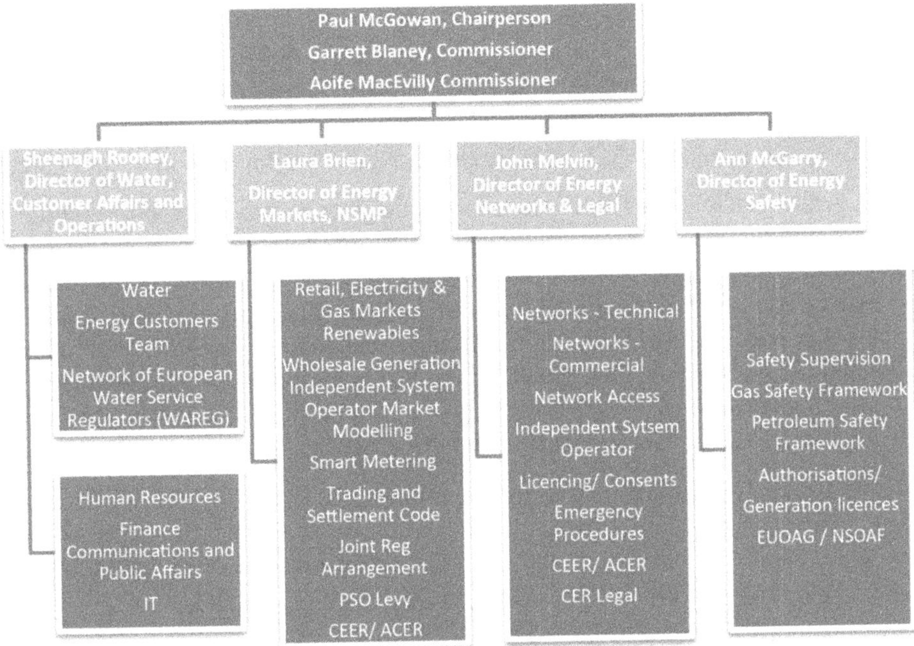

Source: CER (2016), "CER Integrated Business Plan: Year 2017", Internal Report for Management Team, December.

The lack of separate Divisions for corporate or cross-cutting functions to date is not viewed as hindering operations as staff appear to communicate fluidly and efficiently across Divisions. CRU management and staff are able to access HR, finance, customer affairs and legal personnel directly, irrespective of the vertical structure. However, it is unclear whether Directors in charge of overseeing cross-cutting functions as well as sectoral functions would benefit from a more distinctive separation of responsibilities as the functions of the CRU continue to increase. More analysis is required to stress-test whether CRU would benefit from having corporate HR and Legal functions separated from any substantive work stream. Going forward, given the evolution of workloads and the need for specialised professional leadership for all areas of technical and corporate functions, this structure may need to be revised.

The CRU's Energy Safety function – which has its own Division and Director, is increasingly being embedded into CRU functions pertaining to licence issuing in other Divisions. For example, the CRU issues an overall licence for gas suppliers, which is underpinned by a mandatory safety case.

There is potentially a conflict of interest in the Safety vs. Economic functions of the CRU, although this does not yet appear to have occurred. According to the ALARP Guidance (2016), the CER is first required to undertake a detailed assessment demonstrating that safety risks are managed to an appropriate level (including the costs of implementing the necessary safety measures). Where the outcome of such an assessment is inconclusive, the ALARP guidance requires the application of a Precautionary Principle is applied to assessment decisions, whereby "safety is expected to take precedence over economic considerations" and that "in this decision context, the decision could have significant economic consequences to an organisation in conjunction with the safety implications" (ALARP, 2016: 18).

Strategy and planning

The Commissioners set and approve the Strategic Plan of the CRU, in consultation with the Senior Management Team (SMT). There are regular strategy meetings involving Commissioners only, and an SMT meeting involving both Commissioners and Directors.

The CRU strives to focus its operation and management processes on creating a link between its medium-term strategy planning (the active Strategic Plan is for the period 2014-18), annual and quarterly work planning and reporting – including linking personal objectives to CRU strategic goals. Based on its Strategic Plan, the CRU drafts annual work plans that are presented to the Minister and parliament. The annual plan is based on divisional annual work plans, that are elaborated using a mixture of top-down (parameters set by senior management) and bottom-up (business plans generated by managers responsible for delivering specific work items.) approaches.

As stated in the CRU's Strategic Plan, the Commission is in the process of introducing an Integrated Business Planning Process, which aims to provide clear linkages between strategy, risk, resources, work plans and reporting processes. The annual plan includes the following components (is finalised in December):

- Baseline work plan (to be reported to the Minister on 30 November)
- Human resources plan
- Budget

As part of this Integrated Business Planning, the CRU will break down the annual business plan into quarters and conduct *ex post* monitoring and implementation, meaning that Managers will have four opportunities to assess whether the business plan is on track, and make adjustments as needed in an iterative exercise. Managers will need to estimate staff resource time per project / output to help set more realistic deliverables and timelines. CRU will also make estimations of the levies to be collected from industry over a three-year period which, beyond supporting longer-term financial planning, will improve the CRU's financial transparency and help industry anticipate coming costs. It is hoped that the Integrated Business Plan will continue to improve target-setting within yearly work programme and better project management outcomes.

Accountability

The Commissioners are accountable to parliament. Formal and structured accountability mechanisms include submission of annual work plans and reports to parliament (which are submitted to the Oireachtas via the relevant Minister). The annual report describes the work delivered by the CRU over that calendar year with reference to the targets set in its annual work plan. Annual plans are published on the CRU website. The CRU is also subject to more ad hoc correspondence, presentations and questioning by the Oireachtas committees responsible for energy and water sectoral policy. All Oireachtas committee meetings are open to the public and recorded.

At the parliamentary level, the Joint Committee on the Future Funding of Domestic Water Services was disbanded following the publication of the April report. Going forward, the main standing committees to which CRU shall report its activities are the Committee on Housing, Planning and Local Government (the standing committee for the Department with oversight of Irish Water) and the Committee on Communications,

Climate Action and Environment (newly set up in September 2016). This Committee is relatively new and is still defining its role and responsibility. Given the highly technical work of the CRU, the Committee would likely require more help from the CRU in terms of language simplification and explanations to better understand the CRU's work and provide the appropriate level of accountability oversight. The Committee has expressed a need for more capacity to analyse highly technical issues.

The CRU keeps financial accounts and these are audited each year by the Comptroller and Auditor General. The accounts are also laid before the Oireachtas and published each year as part of the annual report.

The Commission has also established an Audit and Risk Committee which reports regularly to the Commission. The Management Accounts are presented every quarter by the Finance Manager to the Commissioners. As provided under the Code of Practice for Governance of State Bodies: The Commission has a duty to act in the public interest. The Audit Committee has a particular role, acting independently of the management of the CRU, to ensure the interests of Government and other stakeholders are fully protected in relation to business and financial report and internal control. The roles and responsibilities of the Committee are set out in a written charter.

The CRU is governed by existing relevant government wide legislation with regard to ethical conduct, such as the Ethics in Public Office Acts 1995 and 2001(SIPO, 2017). Commissioners are subject to a one year cooling-off period during which they cannot hold office where they might use or disclose information obtained during their time at the CRU. Similar rules do not exist across the board for senior management or other CRU staff.

In addition to this, the CRU has established its own Code of Business Conduct for Employees of the Commission in 2004, subsequently revised in 2004 and 2014 (CRU, 2014). The Code holds all CRU staff accountable for following CRU values of integrity, impartiality, professionalism, transparency and effectiveness. The Code of conduct tackles, for example, issues linked to disclosure of interests, holding of shares in regulated companies, exclusivity of service, confidentiality of information, hospitality and gifts, and standards of behaviour. The Code of conduct does not lay out mechanisms or responsibilities for monitoring or reporting of inappropriate behaviour or whistle-blowing.

The CRU is considered to be transparent in publishing submissions by regulated entities during public consultation, including results of consultations and explanations of why certain suggestions will or will not be taken on board.

The online document management system of the CRU is considered to be well-organised for facilitating user search and retrieval. The CRU reviewed its website in line with its recent name and branding change. Updates will aim to improve the website's functionality for users, including improvements to the document search facility. The CRU launched its new site by October 2017.

The CRU's communications to both parliament and the general public is considered quite technical. Clearer language and communication from the CRU may help with building transparency.

Stakeholder engagement

The CRU implements a consistent, transparent and predictable stakeholder engagement strategy. The CRU carried out an inclusive review of its consultation practices in 2008 which led to the redefinition of some its activities. In general, the attributes of the CRU's stakeholder engagement strategy are positively recognised and welcomed by stakeholders, including feedback on comments. In some instances, it is felt that the CRU could take a more strategic and discretionary approach to decision-making in favour quicker outcomes, rather than always systematically engaging in consultations.

All consultations are published on the CRU website and are open to all; a mailing list serves to alert key stakeholders to the publication of a new document online. A minimum consultation period is generally set at four weeks, or six weeks for major consultations. Consultations may also be extended to eight weeks depending on the topic. Comments received are published and addressed in a consultation response paper that is also published online. Depending on the topic, a draft decision paper may be published with the consultation response, before the publication of the final decision paper.

In addition to the regular online consultation process, the CRU may also engage in early stage consultation with key stakeholders beforehand, as in line with best practice, should the CRU decide that the complexity of the policy area warrant it.

In addition to these practices, in 2014 the CRU established a structured stakeholder engagement forum, the Consumer Stakeholder Group (CSG) that meets regularly (usually 4 times a year) and brings together representative stakeholder organisations to hear their views. The CRU presents key points and issues that are contained in current consultation papers, and informs participants of upcoming consultations. In the context of ISEM, the CRU and SEMC organise ad hoc stakeholder engagement workshops on policy proposals as necessary.

In the water sector, the CRU engages with the Public Water Forum (PWF) as part of its overall consultation process on water matters, and initially served as its Secretariat until 2016. The PWF was set up by the DHPLG in the Water Services Act of 2014 to represent the diverse interests of Irish Water customers in the controversies surrounding the establishment of the national utility company. As of 2017, the PWF may be expanded (pending legislative decision) beyond a public forum to debate issues specific to Irish Water, to become a broader National Water Forum. The forum comprises 30 individuals, of which 10 are sector representatives from business and industry associations such as IBEC and various trade unions.

The CRU has also set up a Non-Domestic Water User group in order to update non-domestic customers on the CRU's work in relevant matters.

Appeals

The CRU's regulatory policy decisions can only be appealed by regulated entities through judicial review in the High Court or the Commercial Court. According to the CRU, there has been an increasing use of this procedure since the past five years (Table 2.13), which has made the CRU be more proactive in managing legal risks and incorporate legal review earlier in its decision-making processes.

Table 2.13. Appealing CRU Decisions

Year	Number of key decisions taken	Number of decisions appealed	Status (decision upheld, rejected, ongoing)
2016	25		
2015	12	Non GPA (withdrawn by appellant)	
		Appeal to appoint one safety supervisory body	Withdrawn
			Withdrawn
		Judicial challenge to registered gas installers scheme	
2014	30		
2013	7	Gas access Tariffs (Withdrawn by appellant)	
2012	20	Gas entry reform (Upheld)	

Source: Information provided by the CRU, 2017.

In general, a judicial review will assess only the adequacy of the processes leading to CRU decision making rather than on individual decisions. The court defers to the regulated entity to provide proof demonstrating that the CRU decision is "unreasonable." There is no intermediate option for challenging CRU decisions before going to judicial review, such as in the case of labour or competition courts, or independent expert panel review. In general, regulated entities report that they do not easily resort to using judicial review which can be seen prejudicial to their relationship with the sector regulator. Smaller regulated entities tend to lack resources to initiate and carry out judicial review.

Operators can appeal CRU decision-making processes linked to licences (such as failure to grant or modify a licence) by requesting an appeal by an appeal panel to be constituted by the Minister for DCCAE. The panel can adjudicate on proposed licence modifications. Under the legislation, the CCPC may advise on the membership of the panel, including its duration and criteria. As of the end of October 2017 the first request for an appeals panel to address CRU licence modifications had been received.

Customers can file unresolved complaints directly with the CRU's Customer Care Team relative to Irish Water as well as to the electricity and gas sectors. Complaints can be submitted online, via post, email or phone and they are addressed on a case by case basis by the CRU team. The CRU team engages with the regulated entity and the customer to reach a resolution. The CRU reports annually on the activities of its customer care team.

Table 2.14. Appealing SEM committee decisions

Year	Number of key decisions taken	Number of decisions appealed	Status (decision upheld, rejected, ongoing)
2016	8		
2015	6		
2014	3		
2013	6	Carbon Revenue Levy decision appealed to Irish Commercial court	Commercial Court upheld decision but this was overturned by Appeal Court.
2012	7		

Source: Information provided by the CRU, 2017.

In order to appeal to SEM Committee (SEMC) decisions, regulated entities can only refer to the respective judicial review processes that apply to the CRU in Ireland and the Utility Regulator (UR) in Northern Ireland. There is no legislative body to which the CRU and UR are jointly accountable. In this view, the only appeals process for decisions of the SEMC is via a judicial review, as is the case with the CRU. To address cross-jurisdictional legal issues, the SEM primarily relies on external lawyers.

Regulatory quality tools

Generally the CRU and its regulatory processes are positively regarded as transparent and predictable by stakeholders.

The CRU is not required by law to carry out *ex ante* assessment of cost and benefits, although the Government Policy Statement on Sectoral Economic Regulation (2013) recommends the use of Regulatory Impact Assessments (RIAs) where certain conditions apply, such as in the case of significant policy changes. As per this recommendation, the CRU has implemented RIAs on a pilot basis for certain cases, such as the National Smart Metering programme, the Integrated Single Electricity Market, or the Twinning of the Southwest Scotland Onshore System. In these cases, RIA has been carried out by the relevant project teams, with the support of external advisors. Industry stakeholders suggest a more systematic use of RIA would help improve transparency and understanding of the impacts of the CRU's work as well as major decisions undertaken by the CRU. The CRU is committed to continuing to use RIA as a tool where appropriate.

The CRU is not required by law to carry out *ex post* assessments of its regulatory activities, but it carries out *ex post* assessments of Irish Water's performance against the CRU's decisions regarding its allowed revenue. CRU also carries out *ex post* assessment of revenue and investment levels as part of the electricity and gas price control processes.

The legal team advises on licensing and compliance issues relating to the areas of supervision under the CRU's remit, as well as internal legal requirements for the CRU including procurement, contract negotiations and contract review.

The SEMC has undertaken RIA for major policy changes, although it is not otherwise used systematically for all decisions. Key decisions do tend to include an *ex ante* impact assessment, albeit on an informal basis.

Output and outcome

Assessing the performance of regulated entities

The CRU holds power to request and collect a large amount of information from regulated energy entities. Licenced suppliers that account for over 5% of market share are required to report a full set of data to the CRU, while those who account for 1-5% of market share report limited data. The main challenge is getting data from small suppliers that account for less than 1% of market share, as they are not required to report to the CRU.

The CRU's demands for data are generally not considered to be overly burdensome by regulated entities, although some doubt whether the information is used effectively to achieve policy objectives and whether the CRU processes to respond to requests for information through the Freedom of Information Act treat sensitive information submitted by regulated entities with due confidentiality.

Up to now, the CRU is primarily analysing aggregated market data to deliver better information to the broader industry and external stakeholders, although the CRU is starting to collect disaggregated data – for example on the types of contracts held by customers – and plan to follow up with more analysis.

The CRU does not publish information it collects in relation to safety or performance reports from regulated energy entities, although this may not necessarily be undesirable given the relatively small scale of Ireland's energy industry and the limited number of regulated entities involved.

Data requested from the industry includes:

- The Transmission System Operator (TSO) (EirGrid) and Transmission Asset Owner (TAO) (ESB Networks) must undertake regular reporting on all transmission projects with capital expenditures exceeding €10 million to the CRU. Such large projects are also subject to a formal review and strict monitoring regime by the CRU, in order to ensure that the TSO and TAO Boards have undertaken appropriate due diligence.
- The TSO and TAO are required to conduct a joint *ex post* review of performance against development targets and milestones. The results are presented to the CRU in the form of an annual report called the TSO/TAO Evaluation Report. The TSO is also required to publish an annual report on its business performance, in accordance with their licence.
- The Irish Distribution System Operator (DSO) submits an annual performance report to the CRU.
- Gas Networks Ireland (GNI) is required to provide the CRU with data in two reports concerning its system performance and customer performance, respectively, on an annual basis.
- All regulated entities subject to the Petroleum Safety Framework are required to submit quarterly safety performance indicators with reference to a list of KPIs set out by the CRU.
- All regulated entities subject to the Gas Safety Framework are required to demonstrate suitable management systems and procedures are in place to manage risks relating to gas leakage.
- Licence holders are required to submit to the CRU quarterly or annual reports with updates on compliance to the conditions of the licences they hold.

The CRU has recently introduced an Irish Water Performance Assessment: Framework of Reporting Metrics (CRU, 2016) in order to assess Irish Water's performance over time. Irish Water is currently collecting and monitoring data, and will submit the information to the CRU for review and publication in 2017. The CRU is also developing a monitoring regime to report on Irish Water's delivery of capital investments under the revenue allowed by the CRU.

The CRU has the power under the Water Services (No. 2) Act 2013 to request information from Irish Water, with which Irish Water must comply. Pending legislation may also require the CRU to implement an open data policy for water data collected for research purposes.

In the past, the CRU has suggested the establishment of an Output Monitoring Group to share relevant water data between the CRU, EPA, and both parent Departments, although the idea has not yet advanced due to difficulties in obtaining appropriate baseline data from Irish Water. The CRU will continue to co-operate with EPA and the relevant Departments on this initiative.

Assessing the performance of the regulator

The CRU has a multi-year Strategic Plan. For the 2014-2018 planning period, the six strategic goals of the CRU focus mostly on the outcome of the regulator's activities, with one high level objective that refers to management of resources and regulatory processes. Each of the strategic goals has attached measures of success (Table 2.15) as well as implementation strategies with identified actions.

Table 2.15. CRU strategic goals and measures of success 2014-18

Strategic goal > Measure of success	
Goal 1. A world class public safety record > Continuous improvements in safety standards with ultimate goal of zero safety incidents; > World-class safety performance when benchmarked against other jurisdictions.	Outcome
Goal 2. Secure electricity supplies from production to consumption > No major security of supply outages over period of plan; > Support EirGrid operation of the grid to minimise risk of blackouts; > Support delivery of adequate network capacity to ensure that electricity can be delivered cost effectively for all reasonable requests for demand.	Outcome
Goal 3. Secure natural gas supplies with improved diversity of sources > No major security of supply issues; > Full implementation of European network codes in junction with UR and OFGEM; > Improve system resilience in conjunction with diversity of sources, facilitating storage and improving flexibility.	Outcome
Goal 4. Secure, robust water supplies and waste water disposal > A credible regulatory framework to facilitate low cost funding from capital markets; > All customers paying their water bills, and understanding their bills; > Water and wastewater quality being improved, and increased compliance with EU Water Framework Directive.	Outcome
Goal 5. fully competitive wholesale and retail markets and well-regulated networks, delivering fair and efficient prices to customers > Active, unregulated, competition in all electricity and gas markets, allied to high consumer switching rates in retail markets; > Ensure compliance with European target model by end 2016; > Continue efficiency improvements in regulated networks, as well as diminishing market power in any other market; > On-going roll-out of new meters under the NSMP, as well as new demand-side measures; > Reducing levels of customer complaints.	Outcome
Goal 6. Living up to our values > An organisation whose decision making demonstrates best regulatory practice being followed; > Leaders who foster an organisational culture of commitment to living up to its values; > Committed professional staff equipped with the necessary skills, knowledge, and experience required to do the job.	Input/ Process

Source: CRU Strategic Plan 2014-18.

It is unclear if the measures of success count with baseline measures (these do not appear in the Strategic plan, nor does the plan indicate how they will be measured or reported on). For example, the 2015 CRU Annual Report does not pick up on or report on the measures of success that are identified in the 2014-18 Strategic Plan.

The CRU is currently working on its Strategic Plan for 2019-2021, which is set to be launched in early 2019.

The CRU also develops annual work programmes (Integrated Business Plans) that are aligned with CRU strategy and objectives as per the Strategic Plan, but are structured according to the internal organisation of the agency. In the 2017 Business Plan, these five areas were: Energy Safety, Operations, Water and Customer Affairs, and Energy and Legal Affairs. This may be linked to the elaboration process of the integrated annual work programme, whereby divisions submit their plans linked to division targets rather than CRU-level targets.

Key Performance Indicators (KPIs) have been a feature of annual work plan reports to the Minister for a number of years following an agreement with DCCAE. On an annual basis, the Integrated Business Plan includes KPIs to monitor the achievement of goals in the five areas. In total the Plan includes 34 KPIs. Some of these seem to mix output and outcome rather than focusing on one area (i.e. enhance competitiveness of electricity and gas markets (outcome) by robustly monitoring retail markets, and publish quarterly and monthly monitoring reports (output). The Plan does not include information on a baseline or quantitative targets for the monitoring of the KPIs.

The Government Policy Statement on Economic Regulation 2013 requires the relevant sectoral Departments to agree with sectoral regulators appropriate performance indicators benchmarked against key competitor countries on an annual basis. These indicators are reported on in the annual report.

The CRU provides its annual work plans to its two line Ministers and annual reports to the Oireachtas, via the DCCAE which lays it before the Oireachtas. The report is not formally approved by the Ministers, nor is it formally presented to the Oireachtas by either Ministers or the CRU. The history of CRU annual reports is available on its website.

Note

1.   The DfE is responsible for overseeing the energy sector in Northern Ireland.

References

Commission for Regulation of Utilities (2017a), "Overview of Smart Meters", www.cer.ie/electricity-gas/smart-metering.

Commission for Regulation of Utilities (2017b), "Commission Rules and Procedures", approved May 2013.

Commission for Regulation of Utilities (2017c), "Electricity and Gas Suppliers' Handbook Version 1.2", Dublin, April, www.cer.ie/docs/001028/CER17060%20Electricity%20and%20Gas%20Suppliers'%20Handbook%20April%202017.pdf.

Commission for Regulation of Utilities (2016), "Irish Water Performance Assessment: Framework of Reporting Metrics (CER/16/308)", November, www.cer.ie/docs/001090/cer16308%20irish%20water%20performance%20assessment%20-%20decision%20on%20framework.pdf.

Commission for Regulation of Utilities (2016b), "CRU Integrated Business Plan 2017", internal report shared with OECD.

Commission for Regulation of Utilities (2016c), "ALARP Guidance –Part of the Petroleum Safety Framework and the Gas Safety Regulatory Framework", https://www.cru.ie/docs/001054/cru16106%20alarp%20guidance%20v3.pdf.

Commission for Regulation of Utilities (2014), "Strategic Plan 2014-2018", https://www.cru.ie/wp-content/uploads/2014/07/cer14751-cer-strategy-plan-v11.pdf

EirGrid (2017a), "All Island Interconnection Imports and Exports", http://smartgriddashboard.eirgrid.com/#all/interconnection.

EirGrid (2017b), "Celtic Interconnector", www.eirgridgroup.com/the-grid/projects/celtic-interconnector/the-project/.

Electric Ireland (2016), "PSO levy rates from 1 October 2016 to September 2017", https://www.electricireland.ie/business/help/billing/what-is-the-pso-levy.

Electricity Regulation Act (1999), "Criteria for Determination of Authorisations", S.I. No.309.

European Union (2014), "Statutory Instruments No. 350 of 2014, European Union (Water Policy) Regulations", www.irishstatutebook.ie/eli/2014/si/350/made/en/pdf.

Mutual Energy (2017), "Moyle Interconnector", www.mutual-energy.com/electricity-business/moyle-interconnector/.

OECD (2015), Driving Performance at Colombia's Communications Regulator, (updated in 2017), OECD Publishing, Paris, http://dx.doi.org/10.1787/9789264232945-en.

SEMC (2017), "About Us", https://www.semcommittee.com/about-us.

SEMC (2017b), "SEM Monitoring Report Q4 2016", https://www.semcommittee.com/sites/semcommittee.com/files/media-files/mmu%20public%20report%20q4%202016.pdf.

SIPO (2017), "Guidelines for Public Servants", www.sipo.ie/en/guidelines/guidelines-for-public-servants.

Annex A. Methodology

Measuring regulatory performance is challenging, starting with defining what to measure, dealing with confounding factors, attributing outcomes to interventions and coping with the lack of data and information. This chapter describes the methodology developed by the OECD to help regulators address these challenges through a Performance Assessment Framework for Economic Regulators (PAFER), which informs this review. The chapter first presents some of the work conducted by the OECD on measuring regulatory performance. It then describes the key features of the PAFER and presents a typology of performance indicators to measure input, process, output and outcome. It finally provides an overview of the approach and practical steps undertaken for developing this review.

Analytical framework

The analytical framework that informs this review draws on the work conducted by the OECD on measuring regulatory performance and the governance of economic regulators. OECD countries and regulators have recognised the need for measuring regulatory performance. Information on regulatory performance is necessary to better target scarce resources and to improve the overall performance of regulatory policies and regulators. However, measuring regulatory performance can prove challenging. Some of these challenges include:

- *What to measure*: evaluation systems require an assessment of how inputs have influenced outputs and outcomes. In the case of regulatory policy, the inputs can focus on: i) overall programmes intended to promote a systemic improvement of regulatory quality; ii) the application of specific practices intended to improve regulation, or, iii) changes in the design of specific regulations.

- *Confounding factors*: there is a myriad of contingent issues that have an impact on the outcomes in society which regulation is intended to affect. These issues can be as simple as a change in the weather, or as complicated as the last financial crisis. Accordingly, it is difficult to establish a direct causal relationship between the adoption of better regulation practices and specific improvements to the welfare outcomes that are sought in the economy.

- *Lack of data and information*: countries tend to lack data and methodologies to identify whether regulatory practices are being undertaken correctly and what impact these practices may be having on the real economy.

The *OECD Framework for Regulatory Policy Evaluation* starts addressing these challenges through an input-process-output-outcome logic, which breaks down the regulatory process into a sequence of discrete steps. The input-process-output-outcome logic is flexible and can be applied both to evaluate practices to improve regulatory policy in general, and also to evaluate regulatory policy in specific sectors, based on the identification of relevant strategic objectives. It can be tailored to economic regulators by taking into consideration the conditions that support the performance of economic regulators (Box A A.1).

The OECD Best Practice Principles for Regulatory Policy: The Governance of Regulators (OECD, 2014b) identifies some of the conditions that support the performance of economic regulators. They recognise the importance of assessing how a regulator is directed, controlled, resourced and held to account, in order to improve the overall effectiveness of regulators and promote growth and investment, including by supporting competition. Moreover, they acknowledge the positive impact of the regulator's own internal process on outcomes (i.e. how the regulator manages resources and what processes the regulator puts in place to regulate a given sector or market) (Figure A A.1).

Box A A.1. The input-process-output-outcome logic sequence

- Step I. Input: indicators include for example the budget and staff of the regulatory oversight body.
- Step II. Process: indicators assess whether formal requirements for good regulatory practices are in place. This includes requirements for objective setting, consultation, evidence-based analysis, administrative simplification, risk assessments and aligning regulatory changes internationally.
- Step III. Output: indicators provide information on whether the good regulatory practices have actually been implemented.
- Step IV. Impact of design on outcome (also referred to as intermediate outcome): indicators assess whether good regulatory practices contributed to an improvement in the quality of regulations. It therefore attempts to make a causal link between the design of regulatory policy and outcomes.
- Step V. Strategic outcomes: indicators assess whether the desired outcomes of regulatory policy have been achieved, both in terms of regulatory quality and in terms of regulatory outcomes.

Source: OECD (2014a), *OECD Framework for Regulatory Policy Evaluation*, OECD Publishing, Paris, http://dx.doi.org/10.1787/9789264214453-en.

Figure A A.1. The OECD Best Practice Principles on the Governance of Regulators

Source: Adapted from OECD (2014b), *OECD Best Practice Principles for Regulatory Policy*, The Governance of Regulators, OECD Publishing, Paris, http://dx.doi.org/10.1787/9789264209015-en.

The two frameworks are brought together into a Performance Assessment Framework for Economic Regulators that structures the drivers of performance along the input-process-output-outcome framework (Table A A.1).

Table A A.1. Criteria for assessing regulators' own performance framework

References	Strategic objectives	Input	Process	Output and outcome
Best Practice Principles for the Governance of Regulators	• Role clarity	• Funding	• Maintaining trust and preventing undue influence • Decision making and governing body structure • Accountability and transparency • Engagement	• Performance evaluation
Institutional, organisational and monitoring drivers?	• Objectives and targets • Functions and powers	• Budgeting and financial management • Human resources management	• Strategy, leadership and co-ordination • Institutional structure • Management systems and operating processes • Relations and interfaces with Government bodies, regulated entities and other key stakeholders • Regulatory management tools	• Performance standards and indicators • Performance processes and reports • Feedback or outside evidence on performance

Performance indicators

For regulators, performance indicators need to fit the purpose of performance assessment, which is a systematic, analytical evaluation of the regulator's activities, with the purpose of seeking reliability and usability of the regulator's activities. Performance assessment is neither an audit, which judges how employees and managers complete their mission, nor a control, which puts emphasis on compliance with standards (OECD, 2004).

Accordingly, performance indicators need to assess the efficient and effective use of a regulator's inputs, the quality of regulatory processes, and identify outputs and some direct outcomes that can be attributed to the regulator's interventions. Wider outcomes should serve as a "watchtower", which provides the information the regulator can use to identify problem areas, orient decisions and identify priorities (Figure A A.2).

Figure A A.2. Input-process-output-outcome framework for performance indicators

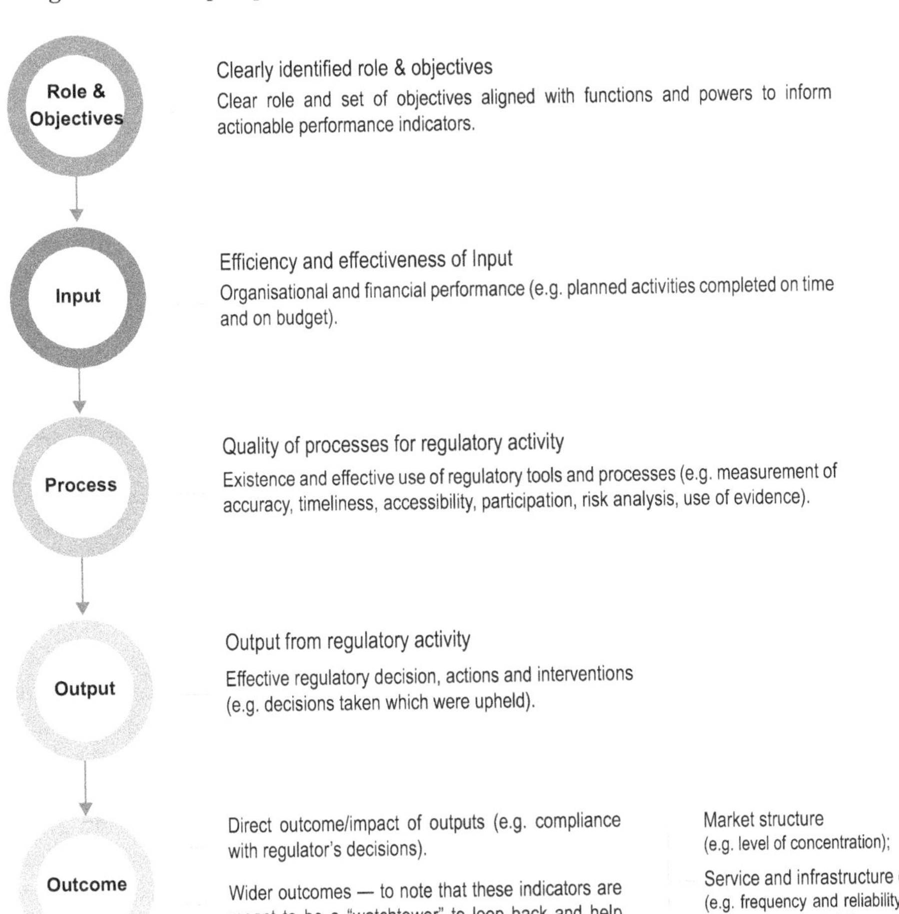

Note: This framework was proposed in the initial methodology for the performance assessment framework for economic regulators (PAFER) discussed with the OECD Network of Economic Regulators (NER). It has been refined to reflect feedback from NER members and the experience of other regulators in assessing their own performance.

Source: OECD (2015a), *Driving Performance at Colombia's Communications Regulator*, Figure 3.3 (updated in 2017), OECD Publishing, Paris, http://dx.doi.org/10.1787/9789264232945-en.

Approach

The analytical framework presented above informed the data collection and the analysis presented in the report. The present report looks at the internal and external governance arrangements of the Irish Commission for Regulation of Utilities (CRU) in the following areas:

- ***Strategic objectives***: to identify the existence of a set of clearly identified objectives, targets, or goals that are aligned with the regulator's functions and powers, which can inform the development of actionable performance indicators;
- ***Input***: to determine the extent to which the regulator's funding and staffing are aligned with the regulator's objectives, targets or goals, and the regulator's ability to manage financial and human resources autonomously and effectively;
- ***Process***: to assess the extent to which processes and the organisational management support the regulator's performance;
- ***Output and outcome***: to identify the existence of a systematic assessment of the performance of the regulated entities, the impact of the regulator's decisions and activities, and the extent to which these measurements are used appropriately.

Data informing the analysis presented in the report was collected via a desk review, a fact-finding mission and a peer mission to Ireland:

- ***Questionnaire and desk review***: the CRU completed a detailed questionnaire which informed a desk review by the OECD Secretariat. The Secretariat reviewed existing legislation and CRU documents to collect information on the *de jure* functioning of the regulator, and to inform the basis of the fact-finding mission. This questionnaire was tailored to the CRU, based on the methodology already applied by the OECD to Colombia's Communications Regulation commission (OECD, 2015a), Latvia's Public Utilities Commission (OECD, 2016b), and Mexico's three energy regulators (OECD, 2017a; 2017b; 2017c; 2017d).
- ***Fact-finding mission***: the mission was conducted by the OECD Secretariat on 15-18 May 2017 in Dublin and was the key tool to collect and complete the *de jure* information obtained through the questionnaire with the *de facto* state of play. The work of the fact-finding mission tailored the PAFER methodology to CRU features. Information collected in May 2017 was completed and checked with the CRU for accuracy, and issues for further discussion were also flagged.
- ***Peer mission***: the mission took place on 27-30 June 2017 in Dublin and included peer reviewers in addition to OECD Secretariat. This mission met with key stakeholders in the CRU as well as externally. At the end of the mission, the team discussed preliminary findings and recommendations with the CRU's management, in order to test their feasibility and goodness of fit.

During the fact-finding and peer missions, the team met with CRU's leadership team as well as a number of staff from across the institution, other government institutions and external stakeholders, including:

- Department of Communications, Climate Change and Environment (DCCAE)
- Department of Housing, Planning and Local Government (DHPLG)
- Department of Public Expenditure and Reform (DPER)
- Joint Oireachtas Committee on Housing, Planning and Local Government (HPCLG)

- Joint Oireachtas Committee on Communications, Climate Action and Environment
- Joint Oireachtas Committee on the Future Funding of Domestic Water Services (disbanded as of April 2017)
- Department of the Taoiseach
- The independent member of the Single Electricity Market Committee (SEMC)
- Environmental Protection Agency (EPA)
- Public Water Forum
- EirGrid
- ESB Networks
- Ervia
- Competition and Consumer Protection Commission (CCPC)
- Electricity Association of Ireland (EAI)

References

OECD (2017a), *Driving Performance of Mexico's Energy Regulators*, The Governance of Regulators, OECD Publishing, Paris, http://dx.doi.org/10.1787/9789264267848-en.

OECD (2017b), *Driving Performance at Mexico's National Hydrocarbons Commission*, The Governance of Regulators, OECD Publishing, Paris, http://dx.doi.org/10.1787/9789264280748-en.

OECD (2017c), *Driving Performance at Mexico's Agency for Safety, Energy and Environment*, The Governance of Regulators, OECD Publishing, Paris, http://dx.doi.org/10.1787/9789264280458-en.

OECD (2017d), *Driving Performance at Mexico's Energy Regulatory Commission*, The Governance of Regulators, OECD Publishing, Paris, http://dx.doi.org/10.1787/9789264280830-en.

OECD (2016), *Being an Independent Regulator*, The Governance of Regulators, OECD Publishing, Paris, http://dx.doi.org/10.1787/9789264255401-en.

OECD (2016b), *Driving Performance at Latvia's Public Utilities Commission*, OECD Publishing, Paris, http://dx.doi.org/10.1787/9789264257962-en.

OECD (2015a), *Driving Performance at Colombia's Communications Regulator*, The Governance of Regulators, OECD Publishing, Paris, http://dx.doi.org/10.1787/9789264232945-en.

OECD (2015b), *The Governance of Water Regulators*, OECD Studies on Water, OECD Publishing, Paris, http://dx.doi.org/10.1787/9789264231092-en.

OECD (2014a), *OECD Framework for Regulatory Policy Evaluation*, OECD Publishing, Paris, http://dx.doi.org/10.1787/9789264214453-en.

OECD (2014b), *The Governance of Regulators*, OECD Best Practice Principles for Regulatory Policy, OECD Publishing, Paris, http://dx.doi.org/10.1787/9789264209015-en.

OECD (2004), "The choice of tools for enhancing policy impact: evaluation and review", OECD, Paris, www.oecd.org/officialdocuments/publicdisplaydocumentpdf/?cote=gov/pgc(2004)4&doclanguage=en.

ORGANISATION FOR ECONOMIC CO-OPERATION AND DEVELOPMENT

The OECD is a unique forum where governments work together to address the economic, social and environmental challenges of globalisation. The OECD is also at the forefront of efforts to understand and to help governments respond to new developments and concerns, such as corporate governance, the information economy and the challenges of an ageing population. The Organisation provides a setting where governments can compare policy experiences, seek answers to common problems, identify good practice and work to co-ordinate domestic and international policies.

The OECD member countries are: Australia, Austria, Belgium, Canada, Chile, the Czech Republic, Denmark, Estonia, Finland, France, Germany, Greece, Hungary, Iceland, Ireland, Israel, Italy, Japan, Korea, Latvia, Luxembourg, Mexico, the Netherlands, New Zealand, Norway, Poland, Portugal, the Slovak Republic, Slovenia, Spain, Sweden, Switzerland, Turkey, the United Kingdom and the United States. The European Union takes part in the work of the OECD.

OECD Publishing disseminates widely the results of the Organisation's statistics gathering and research on economic, social and environmental issues, as well as the conventions, guidelines and standards agreed by its members.

OECD PUBLISHING, 2, rue André-Pascal, 75775 PARIS CEDEX 16
(42 2017 56 1 P) ISBN 978-92-64-18994-2 – 2018